# FISHERMEN FROM THE KENTISH SHORE

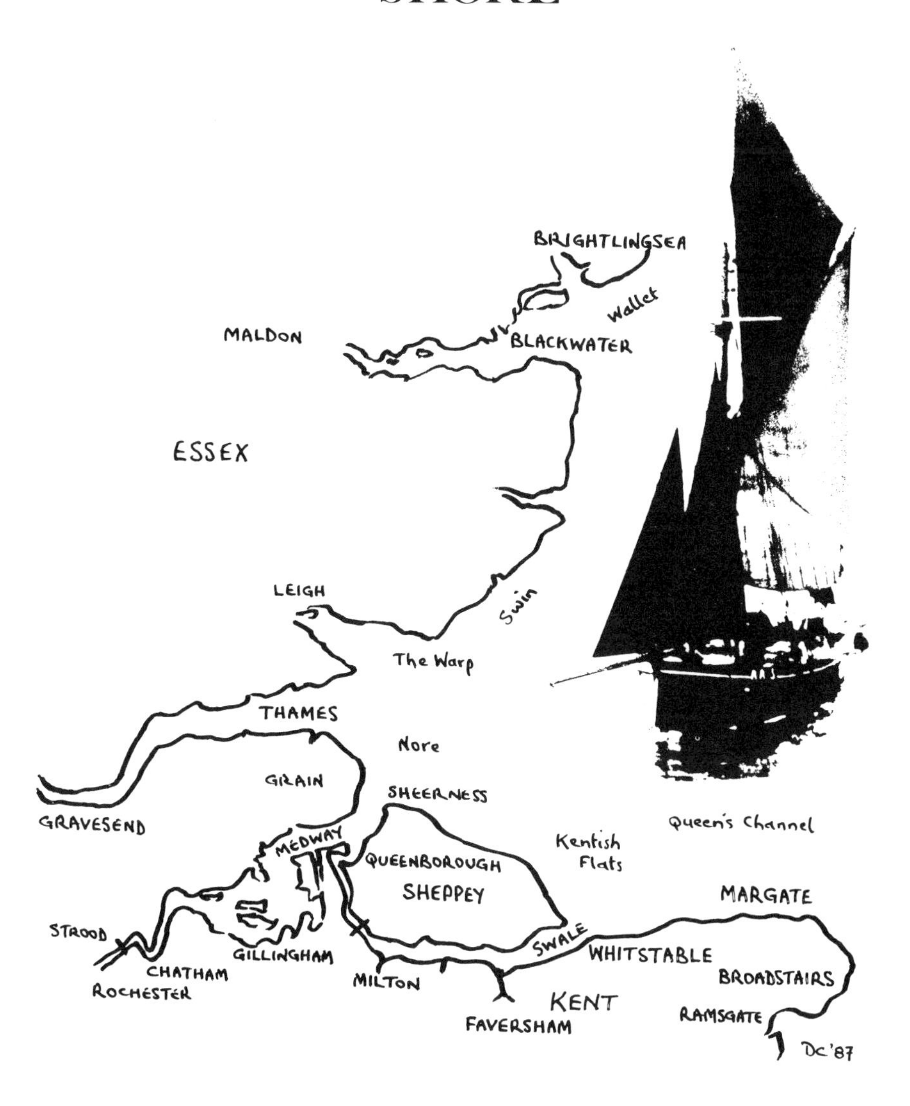

# FISHERMEN FROM THE KENTISH SHORE

*Derek Coombe*

*With chapter by Don Paterson*

*Meresborough Books*

*1989*

*Also by Derek Coombe*

*The Bawleymen:*
*Fishermen and Dredgermen of the River Medway (1979)*

*To V & L*



ISBN 0 948193 40 9

Published by Meresborough Books, 17 Station Road, Rainham
Gillingham, Kent ME8 7RS

Printed in Great Britain by Dotesios Printers Ltd, Trowbridge, Wiltshire

Cover design: Michael Peevers

# *Contents*

# *List of Illustrations*

Note: Some fishing boats in older photographs display the letter or letters of their port of registration before their number (eg RR 1) and others vice versa (1 RR). Although the rule was probably not followed consistently, it was intended at one time that first and third class smacks should show the port first and second class smacks their number first. In the text of this book the usual practice has been followed of putting the letter first irrespective of how the boats were marked.

# *Introduction and Acknowledgements*

The main purpose of this book is an attempt to set down some of the wisdom and experience of the last generation or two of sailing fishermen in North Kent. For a period of nearly two decades now I have been listening to a veritable storehouse of knowledge and I am indebted to these men for many hours of good company. There are in fact still a few men alive today who can tell us about the last years of working sail and are indeed proud to share their memories with us. All can remember the fine breezy days with exceptional catches, but etched in their memories also are bitter winter days when the older men's beards crusted with ice; and the innumerable days when they sailed for home at last, faces well buffeted by the wind and stiffened by dried salt spray and bodies aching from hours of hard labour. Few lives were lost at inshore fishing in these waters, but the work was undoubtedly heavy, the hours long, and the financial return uncertain.

Even in this relatively small area fishing methods varied considerably to meet local conditions. The Thanet men could use drift nets for herring and sprats, while the more congested waters of the Estuary meant that the Thames men went stowboating for sprats and the Medway men used their dragnets for herring. Personal preferences differed too. Some found oyster dredging punishing and would do almost anything else to make a living, but others, perhaps better equipped, found the constant exertion of throwing and hauling dredges kept them warm even on the days when the iron dredges froze to the decks. Practically all Medway men had an understandable aversion to winter stowboating in the later years, yet some Gravesend men looked forward to their stowboating as a welcome change from shrimping.

I have used the terms 'Kentish' and 'Kentishmen' in this book quite indiscriminately, not trying to distinguish between men of Kent and Kentishmen. No one can be sure how the boundary should be drawn and anyway the Essexmen and others called us all Kentishmen. I wonder whether the long-standing rivalry between Essexmen and Kentishmen, which was just as keen between bargemen as fishermen, might have been encouraged by the periodical raids and consequent litigation over oyster rights in the 16th and 17th centuries. But it seems to have become more temperate by the early years of this century when fishermen from both sides of the Estuary traded freely with each other and often sailed over to compete in their rivals' regattas.

My earlier book, 'The Bawleymen', described a number of fishing methods including dragnetting for smelts, shrimping, oyster dredging and fluing for flatfish as practised by the Medway fishermen. Len Wadhams' chapter in that book gives a fisherman's own account of inshore trawling. I have tried here to supplement those accounts rather than go over the same ground again.

As already acknowledged, this book is primarily the memories of Kentish fishermen and many of them made unique contributions to the accounts assembled here; their names appear in the text. But I should thank Pat O'Driscoll for generous help with material mainly culled from old numbers of *Fishing News* and for reading this book in draft: any remaining errors are entirely mine. My thanks are due again to Lilian and Leonard Hill for their skilful professional work on the illustrations. Michael Peevers also gave valuable help with the photographs and designed the cover. Vivienne and Lindsay suffered the seemingly endless clatter of the typewriter, and to them this book is dedicated.

Rainham, Kent
1988

Derek Coombe

# 1

# *Gravesend*

Like other important fisheries around the British coast, the Thames at one time supported a company of free fishermen; no detail of this lives in folk memory now and recent generations of Gravesend fishermen had no guild of their own, although they were often apprenticed as watermen and, after their seven years' servitude, became freemen of the Company of Watermen.

Dr Murie gave a succinct indication of the governance of the Thames fishery as follows:

> 'The Corporation of the City of London's claim over the Thames fisheries to its mouth goes back to 1197 – when Richard I sold the rights to the citizens on their raising money to enable him to enter on the Crusade in Palestine – excepting the interval when the power temporarily was delegated to the Company of Free Fishermen of the River Thames, 1660-1780; but the Corporation retained their rights up to 1865, when these passed by Act of Parliament to the Thames Conservancy.'

An Act of George II confirmed the conservancy powers of the City Corporation, not only in the Thames from Staines down to Yantlet, but also in the Medway as far upriver as Upnor where two boundary stones (sometimes known locally as the 'Whittington Stones') still stand. Evidently in times past Thames fishermen trawled in the Medway on the north shore of the river up to that point, but were not allowed to dredge for oysters which belonged exclusively to the Rochester Oyster and Floating Fishery. Medway fishermen apparently had reciprocal rights to fish in the Thames as far upriver as the Watermen's Company stone at Lower Hope Point and this was the limit for Essexmen as well. By 1881 any Thamesmen's rights to fish in the Medway had ceased but Medway fishermen confirm that their families exercised the right to fish in the Thames only one or two generations back. If away shrimping in Sea Reach they occasionally left their boats at the Lower Hope and walked back to Strood for the night. This could save much time if they did not have enough water through the Swatchway at low tide.

Before leaving the subject of the City of London's jurisdiction we should note the fascinating Rules & Orders printed from 1785. These forbade fishing on Sundays, any fishing at all except by men who had

Bawley Bay, Gravesend c.1880. Some of these little shrimpers show more resemblance to peterboats than to bawleys, even brailing the mainsail in the old standing gaff fashion. The boat to the left of the St Andrew's Waterside Mission door is *Highland Queen*. (Gravesend Library)

been properly apprenticed and, besides stipulating mesh sizes for various nets and the fishing seasons for different species, attempted to stop whitebaiting: 'it appearing to the court that under pretence of taking whitebait the small fry of various species of fish are destroyed.' Also, a trinkerman 'shall in every dark and foggy night hang forth out of his Trinke-boat one lanthorn, with sufficient candle light for the better and safer passage of ships ...' Trinkermen worked a trink net, apparently a small form of stow net.

A good source of information on Gravesend in the 19th century is Robert Pierce Cruden's history of 1843, in which he quotes from a census of 1832 taken in connexion with the Act of Parliament for the erection of the Town Pier. The census showed that there were about four hundred watermen and Robert Cruden noted that there were in his day about ninety skiffs in use but only sixteen of the old style wherries left. From a previous total of eighty hatchboats, some fifty-seven were left of between 15 and 25 tons; these being used to carry fish to Billingsgate from the North Sea smacks. He said that there were then around fifty cod smacks at Gravesend of between 50 and 70 tons and that besides the cod and haddock fishery, these craft made summer voyages to Scandinavia for lobsters. A brief survey indeed which makes no mention of the heroic nature of the winter Icelandic cod fishery.

So far as the inshore fishery is concerned, Robert Cruden reports that there were forty nine boats used in catching shrimps in the river and one for eels and sometimes shrimps. Four of the fifty were 15 tonners and the rest from 8 to 10 tons burden. As the Victorian passion for shrimps grew however the number of shrimpers increased also. Bill Warner is remembered as saying that when the shrimpers spread thickly all along the waterfront there were seventy all told, although possibly not all were in use at the same time. But by the early years of this century there were certainly about one hundred men employed in shrimping in about fifty boats.

Like other fishing communities, Gravesend had well known dynasties of fishing families, with members of the Plumb, Sutherland, Warner and Constant families all living in East Street or West Street. Thames Terrace, a row of fishermen's cottages behind St Andrew's, the waterside church, was known as Bawley Row and the stretch of riverside opposite was of course Bawley Bay. The Warner, Plumb and Constant families had their shops clustered in the older part of the town between the market and the river. Bill Warner had four shops right up to the 1960s, the main premises were number 1 West Street and the others in Milton, Windmill and Parrock Streets. Bobby Constant's shop was in East Street and Bill Sutherland had his fish shop in West Street, as did Emma Taylor. George Sutherland had a shop at the top of Bath Street and 'lijah Warner had his in Terrace Street, this latter lying behind The Terrace which was a smart address at one time favoured by the aristocracy of the watermen, the Thames pilots. This account of Gravesend wet fish and shrimp shops is by no means complete of course and I remember with regret the disappearance only a few years ago of the coloured-tiled front of Filmer's fish shop in Windmill Street.

Shrimpers drying nets in Bawley Bay c.1890. The cod-end of the centre boat's net is badly torn. Anchors on the shingle appear to be the large ones used for stowboating and the bawley moored out in the river has her stowboating davit fitted. (National Maritime Museum)

A Gravesend shrimper under sail c.1890. She would not have been capable of carrying a shrimp boiling copper aboard but otherwise has the rig and general appearance of a small bawley. A waterman's skiff is in the foreground. (National Maritime Museum)

By 1936 the Ministry of Agriculture and Fisheries census showed only 16 boats and 22 men employed in fishing at Gravesend. According to the notes of Ted Burberry, later the Local Fishery Officer, weekly shares for the men ranged between £2.1s.11d (sic) and £4.6s.6d. After World War II there were about 20 fishing boats at work, mostly bawleys but with the occasional smack or ex-yacht as well. Shrimps were then selling for about 10/- (50p) a gallon at Billingsgate.

Within living memory, Gravesend had a rough and ready character of its own. The waterside families had been there for generations and had acquired family, as well as individual, nicknames. The Warners were 'Oakies', the Sutherlands were 'Rooshies' and the Wades were 'Dossers'. They had a habit of addressing each other by adding an 'o' to the first name ('Billo' or 'Benno') or even to nicknames, so that 'Tottie' was greeted with 'Hello Totto'. An occasional fight between rival factions was not unknown, but if a fight started with a group of foreign seamen, known collectively as 'Swedes' whatever their race, then the Gravesend men were all on the same side. On Guy Fawkes' night a favourite practice was to set fire to an old skiff on the beach. On one occasion a group of 'Swedes' was seen to enjoy the spectacle, only to find when trying to get back to their ship that their own boat was missing.

By 1961 only Ted Burberry was left shrimping full-time, in *Olive Miriam* (LO 3) a 37.5ft Harwich bawley built by J. & H. Cann in 1907,

Bawleys at Gravesend during the Great Frost of 1895. The largest craft appears to have a line of ice encrusted along her waterline. (Gravesend Library)

Another view of the Gravesend waterfront during the Great Frost. This photograph is of Three Crowns causeway. The largest craft alongside the causeway may be a visitor frozen-in; she has a stove going which may indicate men living aboard. The rest of the craft are shrimpers.
(D. Paterson)

but there were still about six bawleys at Gravesend, the remainder being used part-time. Ted finally retired in 1965. Bill Warner, the doyen of the Gravesend shrimpers, had given up his occasional shrimping in 1961 at the age of 78 years and sold the veteran *Ellen* (LO 198). He had started 'going away' with his father at the age of four, later skippering the *Saucy Lass* as a young man of 17 years, to be followed by the fast *Charlotte* which usually did well in the Gravesend regatta bawley races.

Both the *Saucy Lass* and *Charlotte* were Gravesend-built bawleys dating from around the middle of the last century. *Charlotte* would have been a 9 tonner of 30ft or just under and *Saucy Lass* a 5 tonner of around 25ft. All had the easy bilge inherited from the peter-boats and consequently could not rest on their sides at low tide so the practice at Bawley Bay and elsewhere along the Gravesend waterfront was to fit legs to keep them upright on the shingle.

Bill Warner, who frequently had articles in the local press devoted to him in the 1960s and 1970s, spoke of his great-grandfather being a fisherman, and this was no doubt about the time that tripping to Gravesend and shrimp teas came into vogue for Londoners. In those Victorian days paddle-steamers brought Londoners to Gravesend in droves to visit the Rosherville pleasure gardens and enjoy tea with shrimps at the little cafés along the front. The visitors wanted to take some shrimps back with them and Bill's father sold cooked shrimps in cotton bags to the Cockneys, as did his grandmother. Their pitches were by the Town Pier and Rosherville Pier, which local people called the Old Swan Pier, after a nearby public house.

It was a precarious living in those days, with meals often missed if the shrimps were in short supply. Bill Warner's father had told him that in his early days they had towed small nets behind rowing boats and cooked in boilers ashore. No doubt fishermen starting out in those days would use any open boat they could pick up cheaply, graduating to the peter-boat style with canvas tilt if they were successful, and these in turn finally evolved into a little cabin boat often with a spritsail (the cabin top still being removable in some of the older peter-boats) and finally into bawleys, which Gravesend fishermen call 'boily boats'.

While on the subject of Bill Warner it is worth noting that he started and ended his fishing life with the same boat, the *Ellen* (LO 198). He left school at 13 to start fishing with Robert Plumb aboard the *Ellen* which had already been in the Plumb family for many years, and so remained until Bill bought her in 1941. She was clinker-built and at one time was fitted with a wet well. *Ellen* may have been a 'beef boat' originally; these were the small smacks used as tenders to provision and powder the Navy's wooden fighting ships. She had a slightly outward curving stem and high bows which set her apart from the other Thames shrimpers, although her dimensions were quite typical with a length of 28ft 6in, a breadth of 10ft 6in and interior depth of 4ft 6in. Bill Warner bought *Ellen* after the untimely death of Harry 'Curly' Plumb in 1941 and kept her for another twenty years, using her finally for pleasure and occasional shrimping until he gave up boating in 1961 at the age of 78. *Ellen* was then reputed to be 200 years old.

Three Crowns causeway in 1922. The two nearest bawleys are *Eleanor* and *Rose of Allendale*. A decorated boat on the top of the slip is probably for a regatta.
(The Museum of London: Port of London Authority Collection)

Harry Plumb had skippered *Ellen* from 1935, taking over from his father when his Essex bawley *Oswald Tomlin* was sunk and wrecked on her moorings during a gale. Harry then fitted the *Ellen* with an engine; she had been worked by sail alone by his father and grandfather, Robert Plumb, before that. Harry's father, Robert Peter, is said to have fished on Sunday only once in his life. He suffered a heart attack that day and thereafter regarded the incident as a warning never to commit the offence again.

A Gravesend-built bawley still afloat is the *Fiddle,* 29ft in length with a beam of 11ft; previously LO 155, she has been reregistered as F 124. It is believed that *Fiddle, Eleanor* and *Lilian* were all of the same clinker-built, 1860s vintage, receiving their LO numbers when registration started in 1868. *Lilian* (LO 158) still survives and is being restored by David Patient. Others of the mid-19th century still remembered are Bill Warner's *Saucy Lass* (25ft) and *Charlotte* (29.5ft), a successful bawley in the Gravesend regattas (as was *Fiddle*), and Bobby Constant's *Three Sisters* (25ft).

At the end it was not a Gravesend-built bawley but the *Thistle* that was the last one to grace Bawley Bay. She was owned and still worked part-time by Bill Sutherland and his son Arthur almost until he died in 1969 at the age of 87. After a while she was sold away upriver but, just in time, was rebuilt on the Medway and sailed again by Philip Wilkinson. *Thistle* was constructed at Gill's Lower Yard, Chatham Intra for Thomas 'Cocky' Morris in 1887, costing £130 fully rigged. She was still a

Bill Sutherland standing beside the wink of his bawley *Betty* (LO 96) c.1930. Thomas 'Dommer' Eaves is on his right. There is an old-style trim tram across the deck in front. (A. Sutherland)

handsome sight in Bawley Bay during the 1960s, kept by the Sutherland family in almost full sailing rig, which was helpful to Philip when he had to reconstruct her gear. Although stowboating for sprats finished on the Medway much sooner than on the Thames, *Thistle* had in fact been employed for this purpose by her one-time owner Tom Pocock of Chatham.

I was fortunate in being able to talk to several men who had experienced stowboating, first Bert Letley at Gillingham, whose family had used *Iverna* many years previously, probably no later than the 1920s; then at Gravesend there were Charlie Bright, Harry Lear and Alan Sutherland, the last having been spratting with his father and brother Bob on *Olive Branch* during World War II.

I shall not try to describe the complicated stow net gear in much detail as it has been fully covered by Hervey Benham in *The Stowboaters*. Put very simply, the stow net was a very long (up to 60 yards or so) purse net, squared at the mouth by two horizontal baulks 21ft to 24ft long. The upper could have been an old bowsprit spar cut down and the lower was

Elijah Warner on the busy London River of the 1930s. His bawley *Maud* (LO 525) is still rigged with mainsail and headsails although in this picture she is motoring to the moorings with the mainsheet trailing in the water.

heavily weighted, an iron bar or girder with a 4in by 4in oak beam bolted on. This massive gear and the bawley had to ride to a huge anchor weighing over 3cwt and, in deep water, up to 40 fathoms of chain. Some old stowboating anchors can still be seen displayed at Bawley Bay, Gravesend. They are about 5ft long in the shank and the flukes have larger 'pans' welded on for extra holding power. As Alan Sutherland said, with this gear the last thing the fishermen wanted to do was to 'swing the cat'. In other words, the bawley must never be allowed to swing with a turn of the tide around the anchor chain. The normal practice on the Thames was to go downriver on the last of the ebb, wait for the tide to turn and begin to flow strongly, and then lower away the stow net (an operation some knew as 'garping'*), after slackening off the bobstay which if left set up would get in the way.

If the sprat shoals were running heavily the net could fill quickly at times and then it would rise in the water so that the long cylinder trailed astern like a silver pencil in the moonlight. In these circumstances it was necessary to empty the net fairly quickly before the sprats died and the net then sank vertically to the bottom, where the sheer weight of the fish and silt drifting in would make it difficult to lift again.

The lower baulk was first hauled up with the wink chain to seal off the 30ft deep mouth of the stow net. The front, wide-meshed section of the net was called 'the wides' at Gravesend ('fore-lint' in Essex) and this funnelled down to the next section, called 'the enters' at both places, the meshes getting smaller by stages. Next came the 20 or 30 yards of half-inch mesh 'sleeves' and finally the cod-end which some at Gravesend called the 'wash hose'. After closing the net's mouth the stow net was swung alongside the boat for emptying, the cod-end being controlled by the separate line called the pinion. Assuming that there was a good haul of fish, the sleeves and wash hose had to be hauled forward and secured to the boat's rail in great loops by lashings called Burton stoppers. This was done by heaving the sleeves up at a number of places so that the catch inside parted and allowed the rope to be passed around the constricted tube of net. Then, with the use of an iron sleeving ring (the 'ringer' or 'cutting hoop' at Gravesend) hung on a length of rope and pulled along from the cod-end, the catch was 'cut off' into a few bushels at a time. These lumps of the net were hoisted aboard (not usually with the Burton tackle from the masthead because it was quicker to haul the net in over the rail by 'handraulics') and the catch shot out of the unlaced cod-end into the boat's hold.

Afterwards the stow net could be shot again as soon as the ebb had properly begun. If there was a boy in the crew it would often fall to him to keep watch while the two men turned in below. He needed to keep feeling the pinion line to check whether the sprats were running strongly. If they were and the sleeves and wash hose were lifting to the surface he had to rouse the men to haul in before the compacted fish died and the stow net sank and became almost impossible to lift without damaging the gear.

*Probably a corruption of 'gaping': opening the gape of the net.

Alan and Ben Sutherland aboard *Olive Branch* (LO 378) c.1940. The stowboat gear davit is fitted at the bawley's stem. (A. Sutherland)

While the stow net was down and the tide either flowing or ebbing vigorously the side-ropes to the baulks were rattling noisily against the boat's hull but, as Harry Lear explained, when the noise began to lessen it meant that the tide was slackening and it was time to haul. If the boy failed to notice this the sleeping men in the cabin would be wakened by the regular noise subsiding: an alarm signal just as effective as sudden noise in quietness.

Like the Essexmen, Gravesend fishermen called the stow net gear davit bolted to the bitts and extending just forward of the stem the 'david' or 'baulk david' (pronounced with a short a). The wink chain or wind chain used to control the opening and closing of the baulks led from the windlass out over a sheave set in the end of the davit and down through a collar bolted to the centre of the upper baulk to the middle of the lower baulk. The warps from the baulk ends to the anchor chain were called 'emlets' at Gravesend (handfleets in Essex, doubtless the proper word). The ropes at each end of the upper baulk leading up to each side of the bawley just forward of the shrouds were known simply as side-ropes, although the Essex name was 'templines'. At Gravesend the practice was to keep the side-ropes fairly short so that the upper baulk was either tight under the boat's keel or not far below it, but this may have had something to do with fishing the relatively shallow waters at the lower reaches of the Thames.

Although the Sutherlands sometimes worked down off Sheppey in the vicinity of the Spile and the Cobbs worked down to the Redsand, mostly the Thames men stuck to the lower river for their stowboating. Higham Bight, Mucking Light, Hole Haven and the East Blyth Buoy were some of the places where sprats would run. The Leighmen usually went out into the estuary, perhaps down to Knock John or the Sunk; although they were also quick to gather at the Lower Hope if they heard that the sprat shoals were in the river in quantities.

Alan Sutherland was able to confirm something Bert Letley had said some years earlier about having to rig a heavy bass shock-absorber on the anchor chain while stowboating in rough weather. They would take a bight in the chain with the help of a short length of cable fitted with a two-pronged iron dog. The bass spring also had a dog fastened to the end and this was hooked into the anchor chain a bit lower down. After making fast the other end of the bass spring to the bitts, the spare length of chain could be removed and the weight taken on the spring, which gave a little as the bawley bucked and sheered.

If, despite all their care, the great anchor and chain dragged under the enormous weight of the bawley and stowboat gear, the men aboard could sometimes actually hear the sound of the anchor scraping over the ground below being transmitted up the cable. When the anchor finally dug in again the bawley would pull up with a loud groaning jerk which threatened to wrench the bitts out of her. As the hold filled with sprats so the loading on the gear increased, and the spratters were known for carrying heavy loads.

Roland Wadhams remembered his father telling him of days stowboating in the Wallet and sailing home all battened down and decks

Ben Sutherland with some sprats c.1940. He is displaying them in a shrimp sieve. (A. Sutherland)

awash. A senior member of another Medway fishing family was quoted as saying 'I wouldn't send a dog stowboating' and doubtless many that went on this dangerous winter occupation would not have done so if there had been other ways to make a living. On the deep-bilged *Iverna* the boarded sprat holds can still be seen in the wings under the side decks and these extended forward without a full bulkhead into the cabin area. The smaller bawleys of around 30ft, like the *Lilian,* could carry 150 bushels (with her shrimp copper removed) and Charlie Bright well remembered filling her in a tide when the sprats were running heavily. Larger bawleys of 38 to 40ft could carry upwards of 300 bushels of sprats, which is more than the 10 tons in weight; even Bill Sutherland's *Seven Brothers* (LO 46) was known to carry up to 10½ tons (she was 33ft in length with registered tonnage of 14.37). Some of the very largest boats, such as the 41ft Essex-built *Olive* which went stowboating from Chatham, were reputed to be able to carry a load of 20 tons all up, to include the stowboat gear as well as the catch in the hold, but this 19.98 registered tonnage bawley would then have her hull dangerously low in the water.

As elsewhere on the East Coast, the sprats when landed were usually sold to farmers for manure, with only the freshest sent to Billingsgate or sold locally for eating. Harry Lear spoke of the sprats being unloaded at the Canal Basin for farmers at Southfleet, Longfield, Vigo and other places for 25/- (£1.25) a ton in the early 1930s. Wooden shovels shaped like garden spades were kept on board to unload the catch yet avoid damaging the sprats so that they could be sold as food from the local fish shops or market stalls at about 1d per lb.

In earlier days when the average fishing boat was of the peter-boat type Gravesend men had another method of catching sprats. This was a form of hoop-netting, which was also believed to have been practised at Leigh-on-Sea. Three iron hoops of about 5ft in diameter were laced to closed tubes of net about 18ft long and these were suspended below the boat, one on each side slung from poles and one hung from the stern. Each had a 'spilling line' to close the net at the mouth by pulling the hoop to the horizontal. Whereas the stowboaters had to anchor and wait for the sprats to swim into their net (although placing their boats shrewdly from experience and by observing the movement of seagulls tracking the sprat shoals), with this form of netting the intention was to sail directly into the teeming sprats with their attendant flights of gulls turning in the wintry skies of the estuary.

Before leaving the subject of stowboating, it is worth recalling that in the past Gravesend men went up to the East Coast as far as Maldon early in the season to 'stand' for shrimps which at that time of the year moved in shoals well above the seabed. For that reason the fishermen called them 'swimmers'. This is now only folklore and no one can say how successful the technique was.

Bill Sutherland's *Thistle* and Ben Sutherland's Harwich-built bawley *Olive Branch* were stowboating in the 1930s when sprats fetched only 17/- (85p) to £1.5s (£1.25) a ton for manure and were the last two bawleys to do so through World War II, with *Thistle* continuing the tradition well

Unloading sprats from a smack into a scow at Brightlingsea c.1930. The stowboating gear may be seen hauled on deck on the starboard side of the smack. (George Tabor Ltd)

after that. Apart from sprats, their stow nets caught 'anything else that came along', although they never went after that other Thames harvest, whitebait.

It is said that at times in the distant past whitebait shoaled so thickly along the banks of the Thames that anyone with a handnet could quickly sweep up enough for a meal. Cetainly the 'baiters originally fished upriver at least as far as Greenwich, where the famous Ministerial whitebait suppers were held in Pitt the Younger's day. Dr Murie quoted an 1885 study of Thames whitebait which showed that the shoals were composed mainly of the fry of sprats and herring. He said: 'fishermen well know that their best "spratty stuff" is obtained in the forepart of the season, the relatively inferior "yawling* material" about midsummer or later on.' In Dr Murie's time the prime place for whitebaiting was near Southend Pier and daylight hours were reckoned to be better than dark. These 'baiters used a type of stow net but considerably smaller than the

Opposite: Stowboating for sprats as seen by *The Illustrated London News* in 1883. One of the engravings on the left shows how the catch in the hose was 'cut off' into manageable amounts by the use of the wooden mingle on Essex smacks.

*Yawling are an inshore species of herring.

spratting gear. It was typical practice to make a number of hauls in the early morning and then put the catch on the business trains to London because whitebait was a highly perishable catch before refrigeration. Dr Murie wrote of the frequent presence of gobies in whitebait catches, the Leighmen calling them 'pollywigs', while the smallest fish nettable they called 'heads and eyes'. Incidentally, gobies have a slightly different name at Gravesend where they are still called 'pollwigs', and on the Medway the fishermen use either the same word or 'pollwings', or even 'pollywinks'.

When Dr Murie was writing at around the turn of the century Thames fishermen upriver lowered small square-framed nets into the path of the dense whitebait shoals drifting up and down with the tides. By the early 1930s the whitebait fishery was entirely centred on Leigh-on-Sea where William Joseph Young owned a number of motorised bawleys. According to the trade press of that period, 800 tons of whitebait were landed during a 10 months season from October to July. These boats were still using the traditional stow net gear and indeed Young's still had two boats to be seen standing for whitebait off Holehaven right up to the mid 1960s.

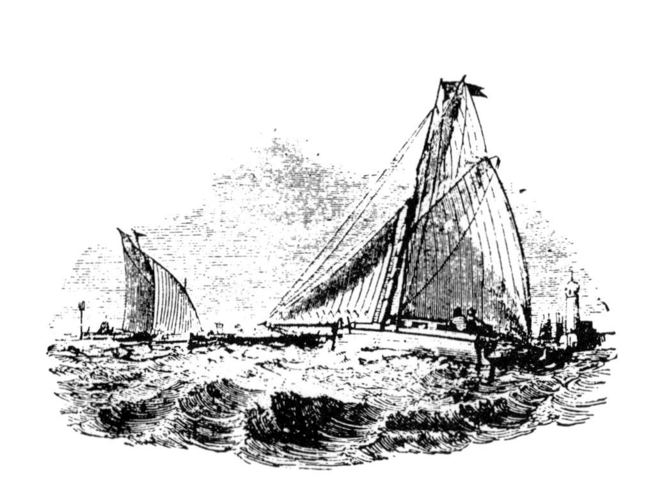

# 2

# *Gravesend: The Shrimpers*

However bawley boats got their name we can be sure that it was not by a corruption of 'boiler-boat'. Thames Estuary fishermen invariably seemed to call their shrimp cauldrons 'coppers', the old household name, and I have been told on many different occasions that earlier generations of fishermen had told their sons that their boats were called bawleys (or perhaps some other name sounding rather similar) well before coppers were fitted aboard. It has only served to confuse that at Gravesend, and nowhere else in North Kent, you may still hear men of the old fishing families speak of 'the old boily boats'.

The early bawleys, like the peter-boats which still survived, often had wet-wells built athwart the hull and these were used to keep the first caught shrimps fresh until they could be boiled ashore. Charlie Bright, who started his fishing life with his grandfather Bill Sutherland just after World War I, recalled that their old bawley, the *Lion,* had her wet-well still. In earlier times the catches were carried ashore in eight-gallon wicker pads for cooking in shared boilers near the river front. It is said that there were boiler-houses in Crooked Lane and on the other side of the road opposite St Andrew's Church on Bawley Bay.

The last generation of Gravesend fishermen were almost solely concerned with shrimping, although not despising such fish and lobsters as came up in the trim tram net. Lobsters were not particularly valued even in the 1920s and the fishermen's children were sometimes given a lobster out of the family shop window to provide tea-time sandwiches. Soles were marketable but flounders were often thrown away. Sometimes the shrimp net brought up a gallon or so of large prawns and these were so highly prized that they never appeared in the fish shop windows at all. Ron Warner's grandfather, Elias Lacy Warner, owned nine bawleys at one time, crewed mainly by members of the family, but Ron's father, Bill Warner, in one of the many interviews he gave for local newspapers said that as a small boy 'I used to stand outside no. 1 West Street. A lady used to give me a penny or two to go and get her a pint of stout. I spent the penny on hot baked potatoes from a stall kept by an Italian near the ferry. Little did I dream when I stood outside that shop that one day I would be its owner, with a fleet of bawleys of my own.' The shrimp and fish shop at 1 West Street was at that time owned by the Sandford family and at 17 years of age Bill started to skipper the *Saucy Lass,* one of four bawleys owned by the Sandfords. Eventually Bill Warner bought the shop and bawley boats from them and so started a

Ben Sutherland with his shrimp copper and dydle (short ladle) aboard the bawley *Olive Branch* c.1940. Note the wink barrel to the right of the picture. (A. Sutherland)

Ben Sutherland spreading cooked shrimps on the driers. His sons Alan and Robert are culling out any remaining small fish or crabs that have been cooked with the shrimps. Shrimps must be quite dry and cool before they can be tipped into sacks and taken ashore. C.1940.
(A. Sutherland)

prosperous business of his own, at one stage owning five boats and three shops. Partly that prosperity was due to Rosherville Gardens which at the turn of the century was a noted destination of Cockneys bent on a day's pleasure. Besides having its own railway station, Rosherville was served by paddle-steamers from London. The Gardens supported a row of small cafés overlooking the river which served 'shrimp teas': mainly brown shrimps, bread and butter and a pot of tea, all for a few pennies.

Bill Warner was the first Gravesend man able to afford an engine for one of his boats. This was the *Moss Rose,* in 1916. Bill was able to use it soon after to go quickly to the rescue of another fisherman, Nobby Shuttlewood, who had tumbled overboard. He was below the surface when Bill arrived on the scene but bubbles rising showed his position; he was fished out with a boathook through the collar of his coat and revived on deck. The story includes the embellishment that Nobby, who was proud of his well-polished shoes, always carried a tin of boot polish in his breast pocket. On this occasion, the tin, being half used, floated up as well, further proof of Nobby's submerged position.

The *Moss Rose* was hit by a sailing barge in Sea Reach one foggy day and Bill Warner (junior) and his mate 'Tottie' Wakefield jumped to safety aboard the barge as the bawley sank. The PLA wanted the wreck shifted so the Warner family got some suitable lifting gear and raised *Moss Rose* between two other bawleys. When she was securely slung between the two on cables they had to decide what to do next. Uncle 'lijah advised running the *Moss Rose* up on the shore nearby for patching, but the rest of the family were in favour of motoring back up to Gravesend straight away. All went well until a pleasure steamer came by with a huge wash. The strain was too much for *Moss Rose* in her fragile state and she broke up.

'lijah Warner and his long-time mate Jim Bradford are well remembered, as is 'lijah's shop on the corner of Terrace and Cross Streets. Up to about the time of World War I, 'lijah had worked with a veteran sailing bawley without an engine called *Lass of Kent* (evidently almost as popular a name in Victorian times as *Moss Rose*). In later years he had the ex-Leigh bawley *Walter Harvey* (LO 525) whose name he changed to *Maud* after his daughter. Notable for her stately rate of progress under power she was usually the last of the Gravesend fleet of shrimpers to straggle home. 'lijah continued fishing until he was well into his seventies.

Bill Warner senior had learnt the knack of being able to find his way downriver and back again in almost any foggy weather. Ron remembers his father taking them down to the Blyth Sand in a fog so thick that it had even stopped the pilot boats. Bill had used both his compass and his vast knowledge of the river unerringly; and he was also confident that no steamers would be attempting to move about in that peasouper.

Another incident that Ron remembers vividly was the time when his father and he were shrimping off Southend in the 31ft ex-yacht *Amy* (LO 82) fitted with an Ailsa Craig diesel engine. An old bass cord cockle bag wrapped itself around the propeller and Ron had to strip off and hang under the boat's counter stern while he cut away the tangle. This

Elijah Warner and his mate Jim Bradford (carrying sack of shrimps) about to enter 'lijah's shop in Terrace Street in 1936. (Topham)

Jim Bradford with trim tram trawl in 1936. The stanchion and bail stick are in place extending the mouth of the net. (Topham)

was uncomfortable because the pitching movement of the stationary hull brought the overhang down sharply on his head several times.

Sometimes on 'turnover tides' several of the shrimpers left Gravesend at around noon and would fetch Hole Haven for the night, so as to trawl down Sea Reach in the morning. Bill Warner senior was generally so keen to be first away in the morning that he would get his crew awake at first dawn to row out with muffled oars, starting the engine well downriver to avoid alerting the other boats. This was to get the first haul over Bill's favourite shrimping grounds. However the evening would have started with a fry-up of sausages or similar fare on the stove and perhaps a little eel-sapping from the skiff in Hole Haven creek. Certainly there would be a visit to 'The Lobster Smack inn on Canvey Island. Mr Constant of the bawley *Fiddle* would get out his violin to accompany the bar piano for a sing-song, and as the night wore on some of the men might try a bit of a step dance. The Lobster Smack had only oil lamp lighting in those days and was somewhat off the beaten track. These musical evenings went on well into the 1930s.

Shrimping was reckoned to be best from June until October. Gravesend folk like brown shrimps more than pink (which Thames fishermen called 'soldiers'; possibly a name dating from the era when the army uniform was red) and these were relatively hard to sell. However the day trippers from London liked pink shrimps and they could also be sent by rail in baskets to other fishmongers inland at Maidstone or Paddock Wood, or to the coast at Margate or Ramsgate (to a Mr Daisy), and even to Dover and Deal.

At the peak of the season the Warner family alone supplied up to forty street hawkers who worked the Gravesend and surrounding areas. Depending on whether they aspired to a hand cart or just carried the traditional shallow baskets over the arm, the hawkers bought anything from half a bushel (four gallons) to two bushels of shrimps. Customers bought by the pint, measured out in enamelled tin mugs (unblessed by the weights and measures department). The two-bushel wicker pads used for sending shrimps by rail were made locally in the 1920s, by a man often seen weaving as he sat in the yard behind Horlocks the ironmongers in the High Street.

The largest and best brown shrimps were to be caught in the deep water of Sea Reach between Hole Haven and Southend Pier. On the south shore, on the Blyth Sand, were the 'green-headers', apparently the shrimps which fed on seaweed, the first shrimps of the season and tasting good despite the less attractive colour, and the small 'sanders' which were caught in the same area, mostly off Yantlet. These would not keep so well as deep-water shrimps but if the better shrimps were scarce the fishermen mixed them up with sanders before selling. As the deep-water shrimps would keep for a few days in cold store they were preferably caught early in the week and then stored for the weekend trade. Sometimes when trade was very slack and customers had to be tempted, only the plumpest shrimps were offered for sale, these being culled by using the fourpenny sieve, which had the widest mesh, four old pennies' thickness apart. The old wire meshed, wooden-sided shrimp

Bill Warner and Jim Bradford aboard the veteran bawley *Ellen* (LO 198) in 1957. The trim tram has been hauled on deck. Bill is standing between the ledges and the stanchion has been removed from the beam. Jim holds the lave net used for removing part of a heavy catch of shrimps from the net before hauling aboard. (Topham)

The previous owner of *Ellen*, Robert Plumb (on left), in 1931 when the little bawley was fully rigged. She is lying in Bawley Bay, Gravesend.

sieves could be bought until well after World War II from chandlers John and Robert Starbuck of West Street, who apparently obtained them from C. Aianao & Sons, wire workers, of Poplar High Street.

Heavy catches were bailed out of the trawl net with a long-handled net like an angler's landing net: this was called the lave net (pronounced as in have). A much smaller hand net for skimming the cooked shrimps from the copper was called a dydle (to rhyme with bridle). Good catches ranged up to 100 gallons of shrimps a day at the peak of the season. At other times perhaps only 20 gallons would be a fair catch. Of course every fisherman could remember the occasional time when the Lower Hope was crammed with shrimps and they could catch around 200 gallons in two or three hours' trawling. Word soon spread at such times and the Leighmen would appear 'like locusts' to scoop up the bounty. There was no love lost between Gravesend men and the Leighmen, but the Medway men (being fewer in number) were tolerated and largely disregarded.

During gluts of shrimps Billingsgate wholesale prices were as low as 6d (2½p) a gallon but the Gravesend fishermen supplied first the local shops, then fishmongers in other parts of Kent and sent only the remainder to Billingsgate. A more usual price in the early 1930s would have been 1/- (5p) to 1/3 (about 6p) a gallon.

As in the Medway, the little silver gobies were sometimes very thick in the river and were often caught in large numbers mixed up with brown shrimps. This was troublesome because the 'pollwigs' had to be removed from the catch. The easiest way was to boil them still mixed in with the shrimps: the little white fish came to the surface first and could be skimmed off. (Dr Murie wrote around 1900 that Greenwich and Gravesend men called gobies 'rooshians' which may have derived from their abundance at the time of the Crimean War). The reference to Greenwich fishermen in Victorian times is a reminder of how increasing pollution forced the Thames fishermen to work gradually lower downriver. Bill Warner senior who started fishing with his father in the 1880s was able to find shrimps in Gravesend Reach and even a little higher upriver at Grays.

The Warners often went shrimping early on Sundays because shrimps were a popular buy for tea on that day of the week. Mondays were slack for trade and they often took the opportunity to scrub the bottoms of the bawleys or do some maintenance work then. The Warners' boats usually had black tar varnished hulls with green painted uppers. The traditional stone or buff colour was used for the bulwarks inside, masthead and so on, and some liked their decks a dark red. Caulking was often with 'bo'men's stodger', a mixture of black varnish and chalk used with oakum for larger cavities. The bawleys were put into Bawley Bay and heeled over on the shingle with ropes to the mast so that as the tide fell the hull could be scrubbed off on the required side and then dried with burning paraffin-soaked rags held against the side on poles. When judged to be dry enough any necessary caulking was done and black varnish applied. As soon as time allowed the other side of the hull was treated likewise.

A photograph of Bawley Bay c.1950. *Louise* (LO 138) has a trim tram across her deck and the net hung up to dry. *Thistle* (LO 406) behind still carries a full-sized mainsail. (Gravesend Library)

*Thistle*, the last bawley in Bawley Bay, photographed in 1969 has her gaff but no sails bent. She was built by Gill's at Rochester in 1887.

## *Trim Trams*

Gravesend's unique form of shrimp trawl was the trim tram. Unlike the modern form of trawl, the beam rode over the seabed at the base of the net's mouth, the top of the net held by a wooden stanchion socketed upright into the middle of the beam with a short bail stick across the top. Thus far the trim tram was somewhat like the old Leigh-on-Sea shrimp trawl, but instead of rope bridles it had three spars bolted to the beam and projecting forward to make a flat triangular frame, at the apex of which was a ring bolt to hold the bridle block. The apex of this triangular assembly was called the sluke and the two arms the ledges, but later generations at least called the whole thing 'sluke'n'ledge' or even 'snooker ledge'. Bolted to the underside of the sluke was the curved iron shoe which added weight and strength to the trim tram and this would be burnished bright with wear if the trim tram was towing properly over the river bottom or seabed. Also added for strengthening and weight were two cross pieces of timber carrying lumps of iron ballast.

Beam sizes ranged from 18ft to 25ft with the ledges traditionally half the size of the beam. Alan Sutherland has about the last 'tram' left on the Thames and he has made the ledges slightly shorter because his boat has not got the full breadth of a bawley and the spars would otherwise project out over the sides of the boat. On his 18ft trim tram the ledges

*Eleanor* (LO 134) photographed during the Second World War. She is returning from shrimping downriver with copper boiling and trim tram tackled up out of the way. Aboard are her owner, Jim Taylor, and at the tiller Charles 'Bonger' Goble. (J.E. Luchford)

are made of 3in by 2in lengths of oak with iron bands underneath to take the wear. Again on Alan's trim tram the stanchion, tapered at the base to socket into the beam, is about 6ft high while the bail stick is about 2ft 6in long. In comparing these dimensions with old illustrations of trim trams it should be noted that as sailing bawleys gave way to powered craft, and the power of engines increased, the fishing boats were able to cope with heavier drags and the fishermen took advantage of this by increasing the gape of trawl mouth and putting in taller stanchions and wider beams.

The stanchion had a hole drilled through just below the top through which a rope was passed to hold the bail stick, and to this was bent the upper edge of the net. The other end of the rope was secured to the front of the trim tram by a slipknot which was released when the trawl was hauled and the stanchion needed to be removed while the catch was pulled aboard. There was also a chain running from the sluke back to the beam and this could be used to take the strain if the masthead tackle had to be employed to heave the beam up to the rail of the bawley. The tackle was not much used however as, if the catch was not too heavy, two men could get the 'tram' up without resort to the tackle. Nevertheless all the bawleys seemed to carry a Burton tackle in case of need. It was a matter of heaving the sluke up over the rail of the boat until its weight could be used to draw the tram down and across the hold coamings, the beam coming to rest outside the rail and against two tholes amidships. Then the stanchion was collapsed as described and the catch removed from the cod-end by bringing the belly of the net onto the boat's deck and releasing the cod-end knot. If another haul was planned the net was dropped over the side again, the stanchion replaced and the tram slid down the rail and squared away over the stern.

The trim tram net was at one time braided of hemp but later of cotton dressed with cutch. With a ⅝in (stretched) mesh, it was originally formed out of an oblong piece of net wrapped round in the shape of a funnel and extended by the long tube of the cod-end to about 50ft or so in length. A number of small corks were attached to the upper side of the cod-end and underneath were fastened three large chafing pieces ('liners'): in latter years these were three overlapping pieces of rubber inner tube, but previously were simply pieces of old net. A foot rope at the lower edge of the net had spliced eyes at each end and led over notched wedges screwed to the top of the beam at either end and hooked over bolts driven into the grain ends of the beam.

The warp rove through the bridle block (shackled to the sluke of the trim tram frame) in customary beam trawl fashion. It was usually of hemp bought in 60 fathom lengths from Starbuck's, 2½in left-handed hawser-laid (called 'water-laid' here and elsewhere). A new length of warp was generally bent to an older, worn length of warp. In the Chapman Hole or other deep-water haul more than 60 fathoms were needed and the join would be seen to slide under the water in these places before the trim tram was settled properly on the bottom.

The method of arranging the lead of the trawl warp in North Kent fishing boats seems to have varied considerably but nearly always involved the principle that in the event of the trawl hitting an obstacle on

Engraving of Thames Shrimpers from Edward Holdsworth's *Deep Sea Fishing and Fishing Boats*, 1874.

the seabed the warp would become taut from the stem, thus swinging the boat head to tide and wind where she could lie quietly while the crew dealt with the problem.

At Gravesend the standing part of the warp was fastened to the bawley's bitts with a short chain which led out over the stem roller and aft outside the shrouds and before running out to the bridle block on the trim tram, round a softwood thole in the rail to stop it slewing for'ard again. If however the trim tram snagged something heavy on the seabed ('came fast') the thole could be snatched out of the rail, or even broken quickly in an emergency, and the warp was allowed to run forward and the boat swing to the fouled trim tram. If the trawl could not be freed from the 'fast' by hauling in from this position the bawley could be sailed back over the trawl and it was often loosened by an upward or backwards lift.

When hauling in the trim tram, the hauling part of the warp was taken off the thole and laid over a snatch block pegged in the rail and a couple of turns taken round the wink or capstan, whichever was fitted, and as the warp came in it was coiled down amidships. The usual open top snatch block was employed at Gravesend with the base pin for pegging in a suitable hole in the boat's rail; it was called the gear block.

In very shallow water, such as on the Blyth Sand, some fishermen liked to fasten a broom handle to the top of the trim tram so that they could watch the tip moving along above surface and know that the trawl was towing upright over the river bottom. Another trick was to set the top of the net mouth halfway down the stanchion if there were troublesome numbers of gobies in the water. It was thought that most of the fish would then pass over the top of the net but the shrimps would still get caught. Others rarely used a bail stick at all. As in everything fishermen did there was much variation to suit individual preference, but without doubt the trim tram was an effective machine for catching shrimps in the hands of Thames fishermen and it had two particular virtues which suited their requirements in the busy London River. The shape tended to deflect from the net a lot of the rubbish lying on the bottom, and the 'tram' was also more manoeuvrable than a conventional beam trawl, so that it could be more readily swung to avoid moored or moving shipping.

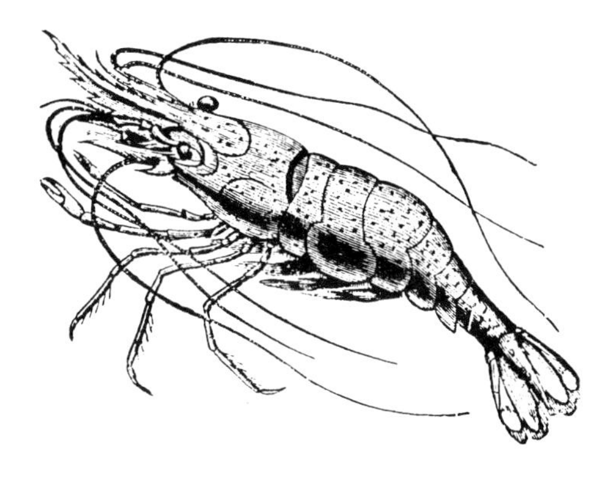

*Thistle* after being rebuilt by Philip Wilkinson, photographed in the 1981 East Coast Old Gaffers Race. (P. Wilkinson)

# 3

# *The Medway*

For Medway fishermen, as for most others, the turn of the seasons brought into play a range of separate skills and techniques for earning their living, although much would depend upon whether the family concerned aspired to ownership of a bawley, or whether it was a matter of using just a doble or even a small skiff if that was their only boat. Indeed some men managed all their lives to wed and raise a family with the versatile use of a small open boat, but in such circumstances they had to be prepared to find casual work ashore when fishing was slack, very often fruit and hop-picking or labouring in the nearby chalk quarries.

In the 18th century there was less variation in the type of boats used for oyster dredging and fishing: most would have been of the peter-boat or doble kind, some with a canvas tilt for shelter and others with a small cabin top fitted forward of the wet-well. For the company of freemen of the Rochester Oyster and Floating Fishery, whose oyster grounds were fairly close to home, a small boat was adequate in these sheltered waters to secure the permitted stint of oysters each day. Thus it can be seen that the old records showing that some five hundred dredgermen with between 80 or 90 boats deriving their principal income from the Medway oyster grounds were probably correct.

All the same, there seem to have been a few deep-water rovers who went farther afield in larger vessels, sometimes down Channel where their beam trawls got them into trouble. In 1533 five Rochester and Strood men had to appear before the Star Chamber to explain their use of an 18ft-wide trawl. Again, in 1622, the Mayor of Hythe complained to Lord Zouch about Medway fishermen employing this prohibited device, which was thought to damage feeding grounds and destroy immature fish.

Trawling has a central place in the fisherman's year, but the last few weeks of the year were at one time devoted to spratting. The old records show that stowboating, the word a corruption of 'stallboating', was a technique developed well back in time. Rochester's great book, the Customal, indicates that in about 1575 the 'stale boats' had to contribute part of their catch to the mayor's Admiralty Court.

In the new year the fishermen would be waiting for signs that the spawning smelts were upriver, for this could be the most rewarding season of all. Temporary partnerships were formed and the men took a

Medway fishing smacks of about 1850 on the beach in front of Ladbury's cottages just above Rochester Bridge (demolished in late Victorian times). The boat in the foreground is of the peter-boat or bawley type and a counter-sterned smack with loose-footed gaff mainsail is behind. The raft behind the boats bears the sign 'Salt Water Baths'. (Rochester Museum)

few of the bawleys upriver (their dobles in tow), and slept aboard at Wouldham or Halling. The dobles came into their own for rowing the long dragnets in a bight around the shoaling fish and for storing the catch in their wet-wells until they could be sold, sometimes direct to people on the river bank but mainly packed in boxes and consigned by rail all over the country at prices averaging between 6/- (30p) and 10/- (50p) per 100.

If the smelt harvest had been good there could be a short break at home for overhauling the boats and gear, including a swilling out of the bawleys' bilges with boiling water to clean the ballast and kill pests like wood lice, and then the trawling season would start again. There were pink shrimps to begin with; they were usually down off Margate in March and gradually working nearer home until by May they should have reached the Medway if all went well. Otherwise in the past the practice was to sail up to the Wallet to shrimp with the Harwich and Essex bawleymen. Although the Medway freemen had a virtually exclusive preserve in their own river (since the Thames fishermen had stopped fishing the north shore), many of them did most of their trawling 'outside', perhaps as a matter of pride. But after the 1900s the Medway men seemed to find less need to work from Harwich in the summers and found their living shrimping in the estuary down as far as the Queen's Channel off Margate. By the 1930s they were usually to be found either trawling the Warp off the Maplins with the Essexmen or down no farther than the Girdler.

Roland Wadhams said that when trawling down there in *Hilda Marjorie* they liked to bring their 13ft skiff on board the bawley to avoid having it keep bumping the transom. Often aboard were he, Josh Wadhams and Len 'Boy' Wadhams their nephew, who was still a schoolboy at the time. The three of them simply hove the skiff's stem by its painter onto the bawley's taffrail, then another heave aided by putting an oar across from the bawley's quarter to the hatch coaming. The skiff was pushed forward along the deck as far as the 'rigging' (shrouds) where it was handy to use for stretching out the net shrimp drier across its gunwales, the skiff's hull keeping the catch shielded from the odd dollop of spray that came aboard.

In the river the larger pink shrimps practically disappeared by late June although smaller ones could still be found as far upriver as Cockham Reach, Upnor, where the shingly bottom seemed to suit them. In May and June it was, by very old tradition, shadding time, although shads were becoming scarce even by late Victorian times.

Soles (mostly called Dover soles in this part of Kent) were often in the river about April time and were good for eating then, although the mature females were full of roe and not easy to sell on that account. The males having only 'milk' sold more readily but soles generally were not so much prized by the public a few decades ago. The soles then disappeared for their spawning, making their return in June or July but were not trawled for until early autumn when they had recovered from spawning and were plump again. September was best, the fish finally going around the end of October, depending on the weather. In early

Admiralty draught of Medway peter-boat of the early 19th century. The text reads:

'Drawing of Peter Boat built at Strood
Length 27.6
Bredth 9.6
Depth 4.4
Draught of water when fitted with 3 tons of ballast on Board
Fwd 2.6
Aft 4.2
Iron Lower Keel (?) 2½(in?) square 5 cwt
Note: This Boat was particularly marked for her Superior Sailing'

(National Maritime Museum)

autumn too the brown shrimps could be caught off 'the Narses' (Oakham Ness and Sharpness) and were working their way into the shallower creeks which were more suitable for the small beam trawls of the dobles. By late autumn or early winter there was a chance of river herring or even grey mullet, perhaps in the narrow, winding, and slightly mysterious, Sharfleet Creek. Meanwhile the smelt were quietly working upriver to Chatham and Frindsbury (their backs getting smoother the longer they were in the river so the fishermen said). In Limehouse Reach there were smelt shoots at 'Quarry' at the top where a freshwater spring bubbled up in a 'pell' in the gravel riverside, 'Middle', and 'Shipyard' at the lower end of the reach where Abbott's boatyard used to be (and possibly Brindley's well before that). Then another shoot was at 'Brickie' in Chatham Reach and finally one at Cockham Wood Reach, Upnor. Most smelt shoots were better worked at low water, either on the last of the ebb or on the young flood, but 'The Slack' at Gashouse Point was uniquely fishable on high water slack. Further upriver in the clearer shallows of the spawning grounds the smelts could usually only be netted at night.

For smelting the dobles were almost ideal, their weight and directional stability under oars were well suited to drawing out the long dragnets to encircle the backwaters where smelt shoals gather. Dobles were also used by generations of fishermen for putting down standing nets, or peter-nets to give them an old name, at low water in the rills and on the mud flats of the lower estuary. Medway men called this work fluing and their usual quarry were flounders moving up shallow water on the young flood. At such times the estuary seems both peaceful and doleful, some might say desolate, when the river's main channel is out of sight beyond an apparently vast expanse of seabird haunted mudflats and saltings. 'Dead tides' (neaps) were said by some fishermen to be better than springs for this work because there was less weed and other detritus swilling into the flue-net.

In the first two or three decades of this century the catch was often sold direct from the riverside or else carried by hawkers around the streets of the Medway Towns. At 6d (2½p) or 1/- (5p) for a string of six or eight flounders according to size, these were a good buy for local housewives with large families, especially when the fish were fat and fleshy in autumn.

For the poorer fishermen who possessed only a doble or else some old skiff or barge boat of uncertain provenance, eeling was a regular source of income in summer. The most popular method was sapping (sometimes called bobbing) but eels were also caught by netting with the smelt 'drags' and occasionally with wicker pots laid in deeper water. The pot photographed is 38in long by 8in in diameter at its widest point. There are two funnels one after the other formed of sharp pointed wicker spikes inside and just below the neck so that any eels attracted in by the bait at the bottom tended to be trapped there. A hole in the base of the pot was plugged with a handful of straw wrapped in rag. The wooden peg at the top secured the shank line on which the pots were strung. This particular pot belonged to Alf Letley, and Morriss Hill

Ernest Hill and his brother Harry aboard the bawley *Lass of Kent* (RR 272) c.1905. Note shrimp drier rigged on right and shrimp ladle resting on the coaming.

remembered trying them out with him once off the entrance to Strood Canal (recently filled in); the catch on that occasion sadly consisted mainly of small green crabs.

One man noted for sapping was 'Deerfoot' Hill (son of 'Beeswings' Hill) who earned his nickname by being a good runner in his youth. Deerfoot kept a nice little cabin sailing sloop at Gillingham and often went away downriver for two or three days at a time. He usually sold his catch to Bert Hill at Strood whose shop had a tank for live eels. The method was to thread lugworms with a needle on 1½ fathoms of worsted yarn or hemp which was coiled in small loops and then drawn up into an elongated ball 'about as big as a lady's fist'. This bait was tied to the end of a fishing line just below a weight and the other end of the line was worked from a light pole which served as the rod. With this equipment the men aimed to keep the bait just above the mud bottom and out of the reach of crabs.

The eelers sat in a small boat anchored head and stern across a rill in shallow water on a rising tide. The trick was to raise the pole steadily when the eels bit and on lifting them over the gunwale they could be shaken or knocked off the bait which was then swung over the side again. Heavy catches of eels could be made in this way, especially on warm summer evenings; 40lb between two men was about the average, although Len Wadhams and his father once caught 120lb in two hours. Len and 'Bluey' Dallas started sapping again in about 1950 and took their catches daily to Baxter's at Billingsgate where they were paid 3/6 (17½p) a pound for large eels and 1/6 (7½p) for small.

'Bear' Wicker and Julian Hill, among others, favoured using smelt dragnets above Rochester Bridge and along the Temple shore but Roland Wadhams thought that the best place was perhaps at the top of West Hoo Creek where eels would be waiting at half tide to cross the shingle strayway. By rowing a skiff round in a half-circle and shooting the dragnet they could literally scoop the pool; it was never worth trying to do this twice on the same day. The eels were sold to local fishmongers at 9d (less than 4p) a pound.

Although severe winters in late Victorian times had taken a heavy toll of Medway oysters, especially in the freak winter of 1895 when the Thames and Medway froze over and icefloes stretched out over the Kentish Flats, by the early 1900s Medway fishermen noticed that oysters were beginning to re-establish themselves in the river. But very soon after they had decided to start serious dredging again 'The Typhoid Scare' had begun. At various places up and down the country a number of people died and the blame was rightly attached to polluted shellfish. By 1911 the Medway grounds were opened for the traditional season of November to the following March, but all oysters dredged had to be relaid on unpolluted grounds or in tanks for at least 28 days for purification before they could be sold to the public. This meant in practice that all oysters dredged by the freemen of the fishery had to be sold to commercial companies or merchants since only they had purification facilities. Thus Medway oysters were usually sent in sacks by rail, deeper shell downwards, to the Whitstable companies or sailed

Part of the bawley fleet at Strood Pier c.1913 with two dobles and three skiffs moored under their bowsprits. The four nearest bawleys (left to right) are *Iverna* (RR 7), *Mosquito* (RR 144), *Alarm* (RR 30) and *Minion* (RR 9).

Another view of the bawleys c.1912. Note the characteristic bold sheer of the Medway bawley shown by the unrigged *Lass of Kent* in the foreground and *Alarm* astern. A pleasure steamer is at the pierhead. Also in the picture are *Mosquito, Minion, Jubilee* (RR 40) and *Susannah* (RR 5).

downriver perhaps to George Tabor's Colemouth Creek tanks. The jury of the fishery continued to give Medway freemen permits to dredge right up to World War II, when another severe winter practically wiped out the oyster stock.

Up to about 1920 the merchants paid only about 7/6 (37½p) a wash, which was about 5¼ gallons, for 'firsts' (marketable size oysters) but eventually agreed to pay £1 for every 100. Occasionally a rich bank of oysters would be discovered which had been undetected for the four or five years needed for the spat to grow to maturity. Any fisherman fortunate enough to come across such a hoard would try to keep it secret. Only his immediate kin would be told and they might try to work the bed covertly by night. But of course in that small community it was not long before the other fishermen rumbled what was afoot and joined in to scrape the riverbed bare.

Sometimes the rich pickings lasted for a good while. The fishery's jury in 1916 organised the clearance of nearly 1½ million of Portuguese oysters which had established themselves in Cockham Wood Reach, Upnor. These were completely cleared out and sold mainly to George Tabor's at Lower Rainham for 1/6 (7½p) per 100 irrespective of the size. When a rich naturally-sewn bed was discovered in Half Acre Creek in about 1922 some of the men were able to earn enough at £1 per 100 of fully-grown oysters to buy the first engine for their bawley, or the younger men to acquire a first boat of their own. Earnings reached about £100 for each bawley dredging out this patch of oyster, this being most likely split four ways: three shares for the men and one for the boat. Even Gillingham Reach was dredged in those days, but surreptitiously because it was highly polluted with sewage and explicitly out of bounds by the jury's direction.

Hard though it was, some men, as Morriss Hill said, liked oyster dredging best of all the Medway fisherman's tasks. His mother tried to find a supply of old woollen socks in icy weather so that her menfolk could keep these on their hands when working the dredges. Even though the wool was soon soaked through it served to keep the wind off and hands remained warm while they were working. Other men found the hauling on the coarse bass dredge warps very punishing on the hands and some went shellfishing in other ways. Mussels and winkles could earn a few shillings and these were plentiful in the past. Apart from the shingly places in the creeks, shellfish also clung to beacons and hulks in the river; the old iron-clad *Agincourt* used as a coal hulk off Queenborough was so thick with mussels that a dredgeful could be obtained by a quick scrape up her side. Mostly though it was 'picking-up', and spartan work too when the mudflats were sparkling and crusty with ice.

One old freeman living in Rainham had neither a bawley nor a doble in his later years but earned his keep by fluing with a small boat, picking-up shellfish and casual fruit-picking in the local orchards. At one stage however he had owned a small and ancient bawley for shrimping. This craft had no copper aboard so the fisherman kept an old copper by the sea wall for boiling his shrimps. Although inclined to

*Iverna*'s wink post photographed from inside the hold (1979). The perforated board divides the hold from the cabin forward (some of the older bawleys did not even have this refinement, the cabin and hold running straight through).

The bawley *Iverna* ashore at Cockham Wood beach, Upnor for a scrub and tarring. This was a favourite place for the job between the Wars. Ambrose Letley Junr is at the bow with a tar brush. A shrimp drier is hanging up against the shrouds.

sleep rough in a shack by the river in summer, he lodged in the village at other times of the year. One of his landladies noticed that her coal shed seemed to be emptying of coal rather rapidly, but the mystery was solved when it came to light that her lodger was slipping a few lumps into his thighboots every morning and walking them down to his riverside copper.

For most North Kent fishermen, in this century anyhow, shrimps were the staple catch. In the last summer before the start of World War II one bawley's weekly earnings ranged between £2 and £5.15s a week. For example, the accounts for the week ended 17th June 1939 showed the week's out-turn as follows:

| | | |
|---|---|---|
| Shrimps sold | 56 gallons | £5.12s.0d |
| Fish sold | 5½lb | 8s.0d |
| | | £6. 0s.0d |
| Expenses | 22 gallons petrol | £1.14s.0d |
| | 1 gallon oil | 3s.0d |
| | 1 bar salt, ½cwt coal | 2s.6d |
| | | £1.19s.6d |

These accounts are neatly set out each week in black ink in a little notebook. Sometimes a few shillings were earned from the sale of lobsters but the main variations were in the amount of shrimps caught and petrol consumed. A net profit of £4.0s.6d seems little enough for the week's efforts of two men, and this money had to be split three ways as a share traditionally went to the owner of the boat who was usually the skipper.

'Setting-to' with a beam trawl on *Lass of Kent* in Saltpan Reach on 30 August 1903. The coal hulk on the left was possibly HMS *Jumna*. A pleasure party is aboard the bawley for the day. Note the mainsail brailed up to reduce speed while working the trawl.

Another account book shown to me of a fisherman's earnings in April 1942 showed that the wholesale price of shrimps had risen from 2/- (10p) a gallon in 1939 to 2/6 (12½p). There was not much of a mark-up for the shopkeeper or hawker since the retail price was 4d or 5d a pint until World War II and about 6d (2½p) a pint just after. Finally, by the 1950s, when Medway shrimps were still on fishmongers' slabs in significant quantities, the wholesale price was 3/6 (17½p) to 5/- (25p) a gallon and 9d to 1/- a pint retail. The prominence of coal and salt in the accounts above emphasizes the importance of these commodities to the business of shrimping in those days. Morriss Hill served his apprenticeship in the 1930s with Len Wadhams Senior on the *Minion* and later with Alf Letley on *Jubilee* and well remembers buying blocks of salt for a few pence from a Strood bakery, sometimes at night just before they 'went away'. The local coal merchant tended to give a penny or two discount off the price of a sack of coal and received in return a regular gift of a pint or two of fresh shrimps.

The constant need to watch the pennies is evident in memories of those days which are still less than fifty years ago. Sometimes the fishermen tried to pass off the previous day's catch as fresh by sprinkling them with salt to hold the moisture; the street hawkers who bought much of the catch direct from the fishermen were rarely if ever fooled by such tricks. But in earlier days there are stories of fishermen improving the colour of their shrimps by throwing a little cutch into the copper while they were boiling and this seems to have been undetected. Another element in the economics of shrimping was the requirement for clean sacks for the cooked and dried shrimps. The Cranfield's barges visiting the Strood mills were a source of supply, traded on occasions for a pluck upriver by one of the powered bawleys.

Alf Letley mainly trawled for pink shrimps rather than the brown, the two species having for the most part separate haunts in the Thames Estuary. The Wadhams family had a good steady sale to Hill's two fish shops in Strood and supplied a number of Chatham fishmongers. Morriss was sometimes landed at Sun Pier with sacks of cooked shrimps to carry to the shops along Chatham High Street, and to Mrs Pocock's stall outside her front door in Medway Road. (This terrace has recently been demolished.) Any lobsters brought up in the shrimp trawl could be sold to Holbrook's shellfish shop or to the Sun Hotel (another Chatham landmark demolished some years ago).

Shrimps were sent in wicker pads by rail to fishmongers all over Kent including Canterbury and Tonbridge and even to Gravesend, the other great shrimping centre, where Edgeley's were supplied. In addition to all these outlets, the Wadhams family in the 1920s had a standing order from Chatham Naval Barracks during the main season for 120 gallons of shrimps twice a week, and were paid 1/3 (about 6p) per gallon. The Barracks would also purchase flounders to feed the sailors serving there.

When trawling within the bounds of the river a good day's work would be four or five hauls, perhaps at Bishops, Ket Hole, Saltpan, Sheerness; and Sheerness Middle if there was time. Another favourite haul was 'Inside' (inside the Navy's moorings) from Stangate Creek entrance

*Minion* (RR 9) and *Hilda Marjorie* (RR 8) tied up to a lighter off Strood Pier c.1936. Len Wadhams Senr. on *Minion* is talking to his brothers, Roland and Frank 'Josher' Wadhams, on *Hilda Marjorie* with Len 'Boy' Wadhams aft. Len was then an apprentice and remembered that on this day they were not fishing but did odd maintenance jobs such as tightening the deadeye lanyards on the rigging. Both bawleys still carry some sail. *Minion* has a stump topmast and *Hilda Marjorie*, although no longer dignified with any topmast at all still has her bowsprit in place for the headsails.

down to Sheerness Pier, a long haul from which sometimes enough shrimps could be obtained for the day's stint: there was no point in catching more shrimps than could be sold. Josh and Roland Wadhams once broke the beam of their trawl lifting aboard a huge catch of shrimps and fish after hauling down 'Inside'.

The fisherman's accounts for 1942 referred to earlier also recorded the spring smelt fishing season that year. At the start they were netting 900 to 950 fish a day but this steadily declined to about 100 a day as the fish finished spawning and slipped away downriver. The smelts were sold fairly consistently at a price of 6/- (30p) for 100. Len Wadhams remembered that year as a poor one for smelt. By contrast 1939 was very good with 5,000 fish caught on one unforgettable day. In the early years of the century when smelts were an acknowledged delicacy earnings could be high. Roland Wadhams remembers as a small boy seeing his father come home from smelting with £60 in gold and silver coins wrapped in a handkerchief.

The variety of fish caught in the Medway in the past is surprising, but the decline in recent times, that has only now been reversed, may have owed as much to over-fishing around our coasts as pollution within the estuary. According to an article in *Fishing News* of April 1932, which recorded the death of George Hill of Dogget's Square, Strood, this old fisherman, who must have been born in the 1860s, had twenty years before previously caught 'a miraculous draught of mullet' near Ket Hole. The total catch numbered 45 score and had filled three boats (evidently of doble size). Grey mullet of good size are frequently seen in the shallows of the river in autumn nowadays but in the 1930s there were some red mullet as well. Mullet are difficult to net since they are quick to jump over or scoot round a seine net if given any chance, but earlier generations were clearly skilled with the special mullet nets which are known to have existed in the 1900s and these were not of the gill net type. Sharfleet Creek has always been a noted place for mullet and Horace Hill once successfully improvised a mullet net out of a flue-net by shortening the cork line to trap a shoal of these lovely fish in The Oats at the top of the creek.

The older generations are also recalled to have talked of shadding, although it is not believed to have been done during the present century. The season ran from 10th May until 30th June and was of some importance to the fishermen in times past. A number of shads were brought up in a shrimp trawl in Whitewall Creek only a few years ago; they tasted oily but were good eating. Plaice were trawled along the Dockyard river wall 'from the ten-ton crane down to the Bull's Nose', until the Admiralty moorings were put down into the hard bottom where cockles attracted the fish. Lampreys have been caught in nets within living memory and were duly cooked and eaten by the fishermen, but pronounced disappointing. Even the occasional salmon made an appearance during the 1930s. *The Fishing News* in 1933 reported that the Wadhams brothers of Borstal had caught specimens of 14lb and 16lb in their dragnet.

*Susannah* (RR 5) nearly ready for launching from the Co-operative Barge Society's yard at Borstal, Rochester during the winter of 1907/8. The separate steerage hold favoured by Medway bawleymen is evident, as is the mast tabernacle case above the cabin top which allowed the mast to be lowered for going above Rochester Bridge during the smelt fishing season. A small area of deck is still to be added across the main hold just abaft the cabin scuttle. *Susannah* measured 39ft with a beam of 13.2ft. The bawley was built for John T.J. Hill for £210 exclusive of rigging and sails. Just before completion she was fitted with an engine and must have been one of the first inshore fishing boats to be motorised.

Herring too must have been an important catch in the past. It is significant that old maps show a 'Herring-hang wharf' at Gillingham in the area known until quite recently as Bennett's Wharf (now obliterated by marina and industrial development) which suggests the previous existence of herring curing sheds. The Letley family liked to try for herring in the rills at Slede Ooze near Hoo and others favoured Stangate Creek, sometimes making the long trip down and back by doble. There were two well known herring shoots in Stangate, at Slaughterhouse Point and 'Shamrock', the latter bearing a fishermen's name for an otherwise unmarked spot, this one possibly derived from a ship's name. November was the best time and the dragnets were used to trap the fish. Even up to the 1950s some good hauls were made. John and Morriss Hill once netted 2,000 good herring near Bishops Ooze at that time.

Dover soles caught in the Medway are excellent but were never found in great numbers, and anyway many local people preferred Lemon sole, a variety of dab. The fishermen would occasionally try bending on the fish trawl in place of the shrimp trawl for a day or two in summertime but by the end of the week the shrimp net was back in use to meet the all important weekend trade.

Harry Hill aboard *Susannah* at Bishops Ooze on the Medway in the 1930s. He was photographed while taking soundings with a pole.

Even when auxiliary motors came, shrimping meant a long day's work, usually something like twelve hours if they were working within the river and more like eighteen if trawling for pink shrimps down towards the Girdler or in the Queen's Channel. Tides had to be worked to suit the market so assuming that a bawley intended to trawl in the river most of the fishing was done at night or in the early hours. When the early morning tides became too late to catch the start of the day's trade the skipper would decide that they must 'change tides' and start working the evening tides again.

In fact the arrival of auxiliary power made little difference to any but the very last generation of Kentish shrimpers just before and after World War II. The early engines needed careful handling and the fishermen were unused to being motor mechanics: 'half the time they wouldn't start and it was back to waiting for a breeze!'

View of Strood riverfront c.1900. A doble is in the foreground and part of Lemon's boatyard is on the left. A paddle-steamer, possibly the *Prince of Wales*, is at the end of Strood Pier. Some square-riggers are at moorings in Frindsbury Bight: these were called 'stave ships' locally because they brought barrel timber to supply the Medway cement factories.

Model of Medway doble in the Science Museum. The builder has named her *Smelt* of Rochester. (Science Museum)

# 4

# *Dobles and Peter-Boats*

Medway dobles were close sisters to the Thames peter-boats, almost identical in hull shape and spritsail rig. It was probably because the fishermen found it worthwhile right up to the time of World War II to net the smelts in the Medway that a few dobles survived there so much longer than did peter-boats on the Thames.

It is said that the peter-boat can be recognisably traced back to Elizabethan times or even beyond. At any rate the beamy double-ended clinker hull carries the stamp of an ancient tradition of boat design reaching back to the 14th century. The name peter-boat may derive from associations with St Peter, the patron saint of fishermen, or perhaps more directly, from the peter-nets used seine or stop-net fashion by the fishermen of the Thames. Dobles, on the other hand, could simply have got their name from a corruption of 'double-ender', but this must be recognised as purely conjectural.

Medway dobles were, in latter years at least, very consistent in their measurements. Of the score or so listed in the surviving Register of Shipping for Rochester, all but one were between 18ft and 18ft 8in and all had a beam of between 6ft and 6ft 6in. They were heavily built, mainly of oak, so that they were not only strong and durable but could carry way when working nets. Grown frames carried strakes up to ½in thick; the only doble reputed to have been built with some steamed timbers for lightness was Alf Letley's *Memoirs* (RR 22) but she was rigged with a topsail over her spritsail so was not typical of workaday dobles. Halfdecked, with waterways and scuppers through the low bulwarks, the peter-boat or doble would have been distinctive anyway but she had another feature, probably unique in this century: a wet well. This compartment amidships for keeping the catch relatively fresh seems to have been invented by the Dutch and introduced in Britain around 1700. It was subsequently used widely in fishing craft, particularly the East Coast cod smacks and trawlers, over more than 150 years until the introduction of ice storage and the use of fast fish carriers to take the catch to market made them obsolete in the offshore fisheries.

As in larger fishing craft, the sides of the doble's wet well compartment tapered in appreciably from the boat's bottom fore and aft and on each side; this to keep the centre of gravity lower. The lower strakes of the hull were bored with ½in diameter holes to provide the

The former Billingsgate chandlers, W. Good & Son of Fish Street Hill, photographed in 1973. This business once traded under the sign of 'The Peter-boat and Doublet'. A plate under the wooden shop sign states that it is the original of 1668 although this seems doubtful.

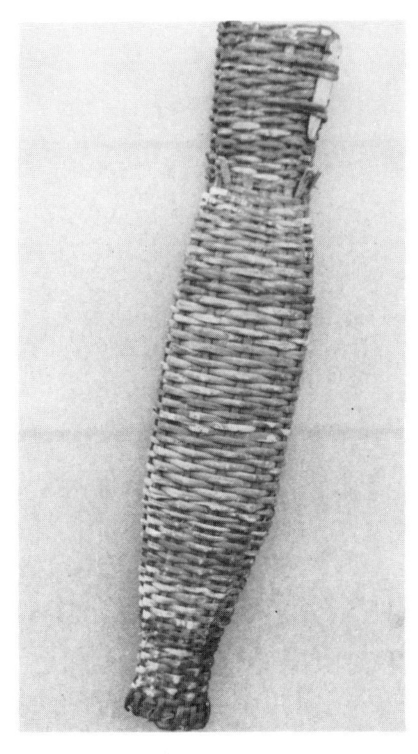

A wicker eel pot used on the Medway and originally owned by Alf Letley. It measures 38in. in length and has a wooden peg at the top for attaching the rope shank.

water circulation required. In *May*'s hull there were originally about 280 holes bored for this purpose. Above the tapered sides of the wet well and below the waterways were small wedge-shaped storage areas called the wings.

The later dobles were all built by Lemon, Gill or Abbott, the very last being *Fosh* (RR 12), constructed by Albert Lemon in 1920. This builder had his wooden shed and slip just above Strood Pier. He was a very short man and a well known figure in Strood in those days. He is still remembered by older men today as being tolerant of small boys who wanted to watch his shipwrights at work. He built in the traditional way, erecting stem and stern posts first on a beam along the floor of the shed, and using only two section templates (and one for the transom if the craft were square-sterned); the rest by eye. Jimmy Miller, who was apprenticed straight from an orphanage to Walter Hill in 1887, had a doble built in 1905. Lemon's built him the *Gladys & Bert* but alongside at the same time built an identical doble for Bill Letley, the *Clara* (RR 32). It was said that each set of frames and strakes was duplicated and almost interchangeable. Although so much of the work was done by eye, such was the skill of old-time shipwrights like Albert Lemon that this was perfectly possible.

Lemon's were responsible for building the light and fast doble *Memoirs* in 1907. She was the first to have an engine installed a few years later. Shortly after that her owner Alf Letley was heard to say 'That's the end

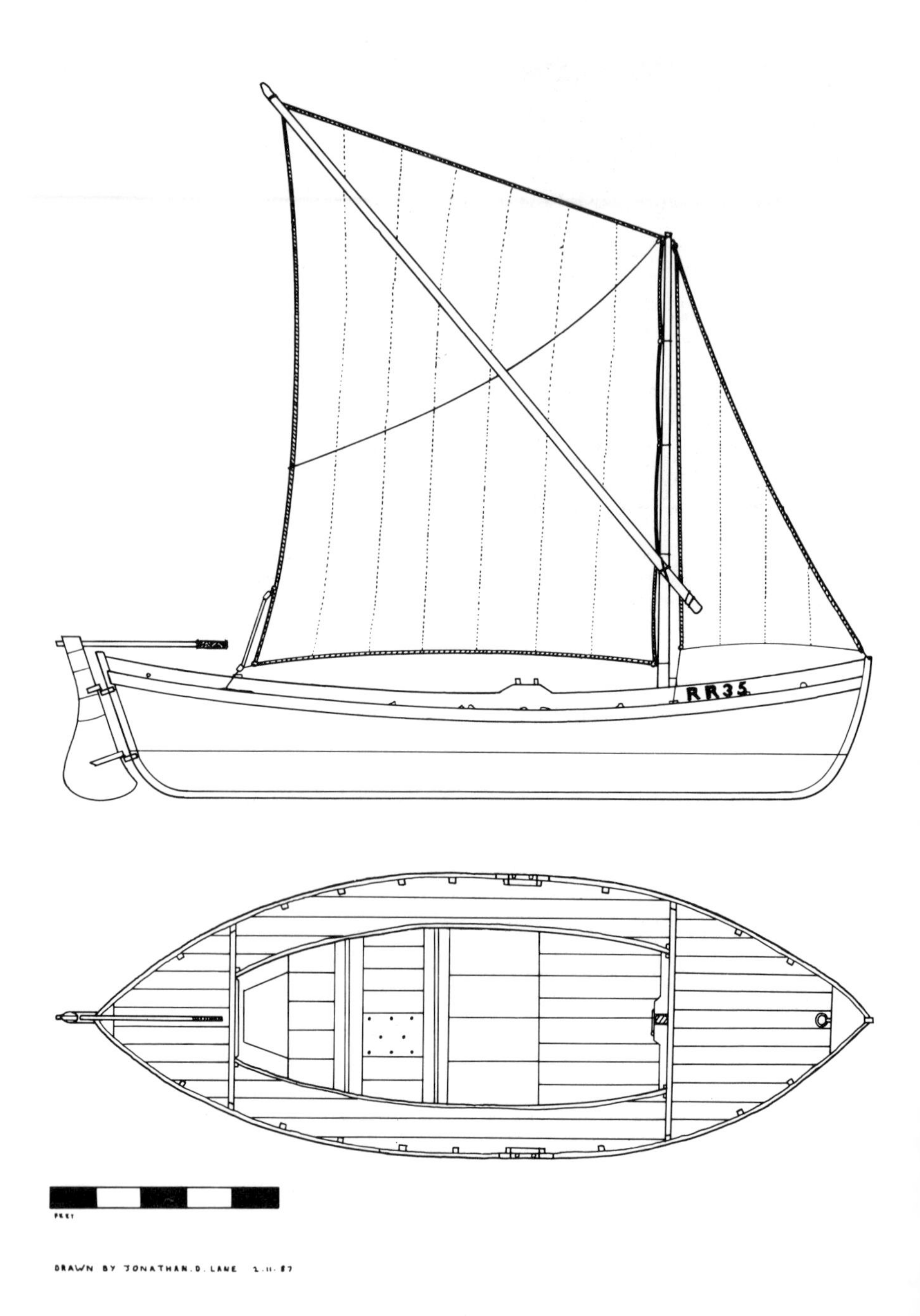


Part of a set of drawings of the Medway doble *May* by the Museum of London.

A rare photograph of fishermen dragnetting for smelt at Halling around 1900. On the left with a land line is Horace Hill working with a doble out of sight — not the boat shown. Also identified in this picture are Ernest Hill, John T.J. Hill and on the extreme right his father, John H. Hill.

of hard work' and started to swing the handle. After much time and exertion he remembered to switch on the petrol tap.

Dobles were usually built of oak and the frames were invariably of this wood, but some like *Fosh* and *Two Sisters* (RR 27) were fully planked in green (unseasoned) wych elm. Most were fuller forward than aft, as were *Katie* (Albert Lemon 1909) and *May* (Gill's 1902), but *Jane* (RR 18) is remembered as being leaner forward and fuller aft and *Myrtle* (RR 36) was very nearly elliptical in hull plan. George Pocock's *Lillie* was square-sterned as were *Fosh* and *Two Sisters.*

A notedly fast doble in the annual Rochester regatta sailing races was Charlie Roper's *Louise,* built by Abbott Brothers at Chatham Ness. She did not have a centreplate however, unlike a few of the last dobles. *May* had a dropkeel through the wet well made of iron plate ⅜in thick fitted with a handle at the top and with three holes bored which could be used to peg the plate at various heights. This plate also served instead of the normal parting board which could usually be found dividing dobles' wet wells down the middle. Ambrose Letley's *Katie* was probably unique in having a centreplate forward of the well. The centreplate and its trunk were removed in the boat's later years, but it appeared to have been the typical wedge-shaped plate of the period, rather like a sailing barge's leeboard.

Only *Katie* (RR 17) and *May* (RR 35) now survive, the first at Exeter and the second at Chatham's Heritage Centre. All had hard lives, the usual working span being perhaps about sixty years, although the *Two Sisters* which was broken up in 1918 was reputed to have lasted for 102 years.

*Katie*'s sprit and stanliff gear with the mainsail fully brailed.

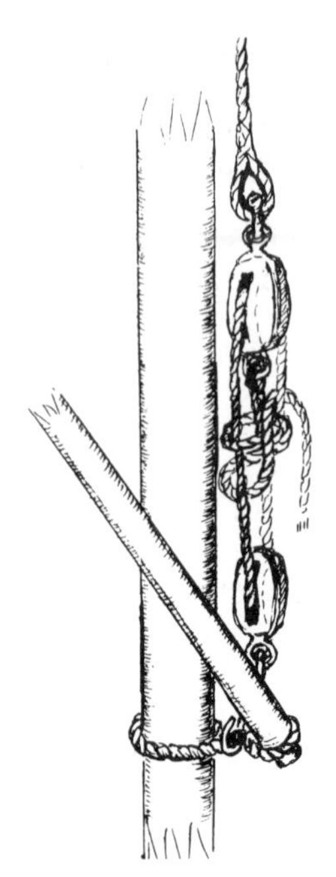

A fisherman's method of belaying the doble's stanliff gear for supporting the heel of the sprit. Sketch by Leslie H. Hill.

### *Sailing Rig*

Masts were often without supporting forestay or shrouds and would usually have ranged from 12ft 6in to 14ft in length. Squared from deck level downwards for chocking, the base about 4in square stepped into the keelson. Unstayed masts have to be stout and the doble's mast was not much tapered; the diameter would be about 3½in at the point just above where it was squared off reducing to about 2⅞in at the internal halyard sheave. The sprit would be some 15ft long and not too heavy, tapered at both ends in the traditional manner. There was no yard tackle to support the sprit as for a Thames sailing barge, but the sprit was set up with a stanliff tackle: a rope from the masthead was a pendant for a double whip tackle, the lower block hooked to the seizing of the snotter to give a fairer lead than if hooked to the base of the sprit itself. The snotter was simply a grommet (and generally called such by the fishermen) seized into two loops, one around the mast and the other acting as a muzzle for the base of the sprit.

It was fairly usual practice to stow the mainsail against the mast with the sprit unshipped when not in use, so no halyard was required. One method of holding the throat of the mainsail to the masthead was to use another grommet seized in the middle so that one loop fitted over the collar of the mast with the other being worked into the throat of the sail. The eyelet at the mainsail throat could also be used for the brailing gear. The method was to suspend a thimble or small block each side of the sail on a short length of rope ('nine yarn stuff' or codline) passed through the eyelet; the brail rope was rove through one thimble then looped downwards and round the leech of the sail (not necessarily through a cringle, it could be loose), up again to the thimble on the other side of the sail, where the two ends were joined to a single rope which led down to a pin or cleat by the mast chock. Alternatively, a double block could be used at the masthead, the brail rope simply reeving through the two sheave holes and the two hauling parts leading down to the base of the mast where they were made fast.

The stanliff might be eye-spliced at both ends, the upper eye fitted over the mainsail's throat grommet at the masthead and the lower eye shackled to the upper block of the double whip tackle. The tackle when set up was secured by taking a half hitch round all parts below the upper block and jamming the bight between the parts (a common practice of fishermen).

The mainsail could be laced to the mast but sometimes the tackline kept it taut enough – simplicity was always the aim – and some fishermen just lashed the throat to the mast without bothering with grommets. The main horse was usually just a rope stretched across the afterdeck between gunwales (using a convenient scupper hole) on which ran the eye of the lower block. The mainsheet could lead down from the cringle at the bottom of the leech, reeving through the lower block, up through the higher block at the first row of reefing points and back down to the lower block to be belayed round the pin in the lower block, barge and bawley style.

The foresail, which was set flying (not hanked to the forestay) had a standing sheet travelling either on an iron horse let in the deck or on a simple rope horse across the foredeck. One refinement was to rig two extra lines from the standing sheet which rove through thimbles attached to either end of the iron horse when this was fitted and then led aft, one on each side along the waterways. These could be hauled tight on the leeward side if needed to make the foresail set flatter, or the windward line could be held when wending as dobles sometimes needed help to come about, especially if the bottom wanted a scrub.

The ash oars were 15ft long or more with squared looms for balance, often with spoon blades about 3ft long by 6in wide. The heavy rowing box laid athwart the boat in the working area forward of the wet well. Two rowers could sit side by side on the padded top while inside there were stored small items of gear and sometimes provisions. *May*'s original rowing box had eventually rotted but John Hill made the replacement to the exact size of the original: length 30in; width 10¾in at the base tapering to 8¾in wide at the top (lid); depth of box also 8¾in. Two strips of wood were attached underneath running from front to back to keep the bottom dry.

Roland Wadhams' *Shamrock* had a good set of sails purchased for 15/- (75p) secondhand from the river police when they finally gave up their sailing skiffs and bought a motorboat in the 1920s. It was a spritsail main

Donald Coombe at the helm of *Katie* in 1970. My brother bought her from Ambrose Letley after 'Ambo' retired from fishing. *Katie*'s mainsail is brailed as she is being brought in to the shore.

A rare photograph of a working doble with a standing lugsail rig c.1910. This was the big doble *Two Brothers* built specially for the largest fisherman on the river, Bill Letley. He is sitting nearest the camera in the stern. (H.C. Moore)

but rigged with a boom which proved to be an advantage in keeping the sail filled when running before a light wind. Albert Lemon charged another 5/- (25p) for cutting a slot in the doble's wet well and adding some trunking for strength so that an iron centreplate could be worked through the well.

Roland recalled that 23-stone Bill Letley had his doble *Two Brothers* built specially big and beamy to take his great size and weight. At about 20ft in length she was possibly the largest Medway doble ever built. Once Bill got trapped when working a smelt net in a soft spot on the foreshore in Tower Reach, Borstal caused by a pell (freshwater spring). After some fruitless attempts to extricate him the other men roped Bill between two dobles and all calmly waited for the rising tide to lift him free.

A doble was the best kind of craft that a young man just out of his apprenticeship might hope to be given if his family could afford it or his ex-master generous enough. And if he eventually aspired to ownership of a bawley he would still keep his doble as an auxiliary to use close to home for trawling, fluing or eeling. But the prime use for the doble, and the Thames peter-boat too in earlier times, was for taking part in the harvesting of the smelts as they moved upriver from late summer to early spring towards their spawning grounds; and the wet well was invaluable for keeping these gourmet fish fresh for sale. The best hauls of smelt were to be had on the spawning spots in the narrower but still tidal reaches of the river above Rochester, but the men who in the early years of this century were still making a living just from a doble did not normally take part, since the practice was for the men who owned bawleys to live aboard at Wouldham or Halling, having towed their

*Katie* (RR 17) under full sail in Gillingham Reach in 1968.

Two dobles ashore at Strood c.1968. *May* (RR 35) is nearest the camera with John Hill standing alongside. Her wet-well hatches have been removed and the storage wings on each side of the well can be clearly seen. Behind her is *Lillie* (RR 49) with Len Wadhams Senr. and Junr. This doble had a square stern. (J. Oliver)

dobles up for the actual business of dragnetting. However Roland Wadhams clearly remembers Ambrose Letley and his apprentice, Ern Bartholomew, sleeping on 'Ambo's' doble *Katie* moored in the reeds above Halling. They had only the sails as shelter in bitter early spring weather.

They were indeed a resilient breed of men. Here is a description of one as told by Leslie Hill. 'Mr Seagull, known to us all as "Harry Seals", was a tough old chap, with a dry sense of humour. He and his wife had a little shop in Newark Street, Strood where they sold mostly shellfish and eel pies for which she was renowned. Harry had lost most of his ears from frostbite. He had been away in his doble alone downriver in freezing weather. Fog came down and he spent the night rowing to and fro across a creek to try and keep warm but was badly frostbitten when help reached him the next day. I rowed up river with him once in his doble. He had put his clay pipe away and had stopped responding to my remarks. I thought he was dozing off by my side on the rowing box, so increased my speed of stroke but he kept in time with me however much I varied it. Was he asleep? I was assured afterwards by others that he probably was, and often did it.'

The doble could be used in light winds for towing a small beam trawl of about 12ft width, usually for brown shrimps. A favourite place was above Rochester Bridge in Temple Reach where the largest brown shrimps in the river could be caught, especially when the whiting shoals drove them upriver in winter. For the men who scraped a living in the style of the old peter-boatmen the doble was well suited for using the flue net for flounders at low tide in the creeks downriver. These fish could be hawked around the streets of the Medway Towns in the early years of this century, a cheap and popular meal with the large families of that era. Dobles were frequently used for eeling. Some put down trots of long wicker eel pots baited with broken crab or pieces of fish but these were not remembered as being very effective. At times the eels were netted with smelt dragnets, subject to obtaining the special permission of the Mayor of Rochester as Admiral of the River.

In winter the dobles were often employed for a few hours 'drudging' on the oyster grounds, so keeping faith with an older tradition when almost all of the fishermen's vessels were of the peter-boat type and the oyster fishery was the mainstay of their livelihood. Finally, the tough old dobles were eminently suitable for dredging up lumps of coal from the riverbed which had been lost during the coaling of a steamship or the unloading of the screw colliers which plied to and from Northumberland. 'Coaling' was the recognised prerogative of the freemen of the river and a useful source of income since the smaller lumps were sold to the local foundries and the rest were useful for domestic purposes or for fuelling the shrimp coppers on the bawleys. One freeman, 'Ginger' Tom Hill, who worked an old barge's boat rather than a doble, never went fishing at all in his latter years but was often to be seen coaling off Chatham Point.

To return finally to the story of dobles and peter-boats, it was with an awareness of the closing of a chapter in maritime history that on a fine

John and Morriss Hill sailing their doble *May* in 1975. Built by Gill's in 1902, she is still to be seen at the Medway Heritage Centre in full sailing rig.

Morriss Hill rowing *May* for the very last time on 13 August 1981, the day she was taken ashore to go on show at the Medway Heritage Centre. That day marked the ending of the centuries old tradition of working peter-boats on the Thames and Medway. (An outboard engine bracket is fitted at *May*'s stern in this picture.)

summer morning in 1981 I accompanied Morriss Hill in taking his sturdy old *May*, the last doble left afloat, on her final journey by water. Mostly with the help of a Seagull outboard motor, but also part of the way under oars, we made our way downriver from Strood to the Royal Engineers' hard at Upnor. The Sappers received her into their care and a few weeks later took her by road to the Maritime Heritage Centre in what was previously St Mary's Church, Chatham. She was lifted by crane over the churchyard wall cradled partly on her side to get through the doors, and with that most effective source of power, an ample supply of willing men, released from the cradle and moved into her place: fittingly the nave of the ancient seamen's church overlooking the stretch of river where Henry VIII commissioned the building of the first warship at Chatham.

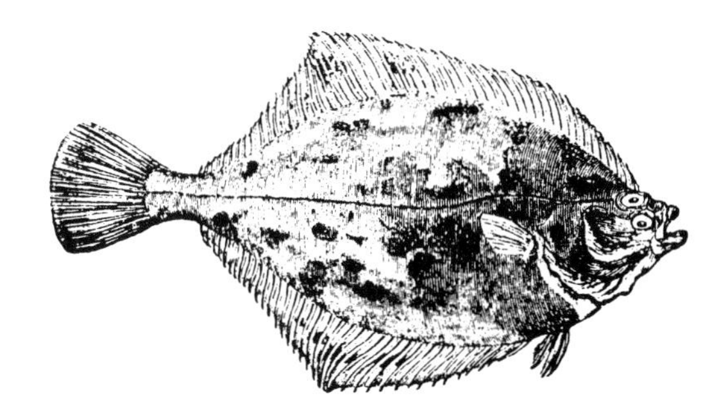

# 5

# *Sheppey and The Swale*

The most important centre of fishing activity on the Isle of Sheppey in times past was the little town of Queenborough whose oyster grounds in the Swale extended from Queenborough Spit eastwards to Kingsferry. The oyster fishery was for centuries free and common to every burgess of the borough, but during the 17th and early 18th centuries there was a long and scandalous history of corruption and mismanagement with consequent poverty for the ordinary fisherfolk. In the early 18th century Daniel Defoe wrote of Queenborough: 'a miserable and dirty Fishing town ... the chief traders ... seem to be Alehouse keepers and Oyster catchers'.

In 1859 the oyster fishery passed from the bankrupt borough to a trust which granted leases for fishing and dredging rights. By the 1890s a merchant still fattened imported oyster stock on the beds in Long Reach in the Swale, but the old storage pits off Queenborough causeway were no longer used. Even so it is recorded that about 1.8 million oysters were sold from these grounds every year between 1902 and 1906, the trade declining to negligible amounts by 1914. In 1937 the wheel turned full circle when the Charity Commissioners appointed the Borough Council trustees thus bringing the rights of the no longer productive oyster grounds back to the town again. However Queenborough's fishing families retained a few bawleys and other smacks right up to the end of the sailing era.

Dr Murie wrote that Rochester and Queenborough men went stowboating for sprats as far down as the North Foreland in the 1870s, and so did the Essexmen of course, from Tollesbury, Rowhedge, Brightlingsea and Wivenhoe. *The Kentish Gazette* in early 1872 reported that immense quantities of sprats were being landed at Whitstable. 300 tons were despatched in a day as manure for the Kentish hop gardens at prices of between 8d and 10d a bushel.

One Queenborough fisherman and yacht pilot was Gus Smith who had a smack *Moss Rose* which used to lie in The Lappel off Blue Town, Sheerness. He went out fishing one night during World War I and was never heard of again. It is thought that he was run down by a ship since he would not have been showing any lights, but the facts were never known. Earlier he had skippered the Gill-built bawley *Francois* for the Chatham fishmonger Frank Raycraft. Out spratting on the Barrow

'Unloading a Fishing Smack', a photograph by Walter J. Cole of bawleymen coming ashore at Sheerness or Minster c.1900. (Maidstone Museum)

Sands the weather had turned rough and the bawley tried to head for shelter in the Swale. *Francois* could not be made to wind and eventually Gus Smith turned her round and ran for Ramsgate. The bawley was afterwards rebuilt forward with fuller bow sections.

Some of the local men had small boats of the Essex cockler type, LO-registered. The four Ketley brothers at Queenborough owned two until the 1950s or later, *Tame Duck* and *Wild Duck,* this latter being fully rigged complete with a topmast at one time. In fine weather the Ketleys took their little boats down as far as the Queen's Channel for shrimps and they had a reputation for going out fishing in rough weather when fishermen in larger craft would not. The Ketley brothers were 'Buff', Bert, Bill and Sam; none of them married but their widowed sister kept house for them and helped sell the catch. Also remembered was Charlie Wildish who had two bawleys at The Lappel, *Early Bird* and *Britannia,* the latter moored for many years just off Sheerness Corporation's Pier in the area known as Rats' Bay. All of these boats carried on the usual Thames Estuary activities of shrimping and fish trawling, also eeling, especially on 'The Grounds' off Milton Creek in the Swale.

In summer, 'shorewalking' came into play and men of the Watkins, Wildish and Jacobs families worked along the Sheppey beaches. On Thanet others were doing the same, and it was from Harold Letley of Birchington that I heard the technical details. Shorewalking was a form of seining or dragnetting, the net being about 10 fathoms in length and used with poles at the ends, to which the cork line was bent about a third

Another photograph taken by Mr Cole apparently at Sheerness around the turn of the century entitled 'A Sixpenny Row Out'. (Maidstone Museum)

of the pole's length down. It was a two-man job with each alternately wading out in the sea up to his waist (or up to his shoulders if he walked into a patch of soft clay, which they called 'pug' or 'clyte'). Five or six hours of this was strenuous work.

Each man held his pole so that the lead line was about level with the base, but it was not made fast, the line being taken through his legs, over his back and shoulders and a couple of turns then taken round the pole. Both men had a fish bag slung over their backs as well but had to maintain control of the net with the pole and lead line as they moved along the beach. The outside man waded round in an arc and both hauled to bring the bight of the net into the beach; it was then the other's turn to wade out and in this way alternate sides of the net collected the debris and then tended to clear as the men circled round in turn. The Sheppey men were usually after 'cockleshell plaice', the fish feeding on trails of immature cockles in the sandy mud close inshore, but they also caught dabs and even Dover soles at times.

Essex smacks (often called 'boomsail boats' by the Kentish bawleymen) were an everyday sight in these waters. They used the Swale, particularly The Lappel bay south of Garrison Point, for shelter when working the Kentish side of the Estuary. In the 1920s it was known to count up to fifty smacks at a time crammed into The Lappel when a hard easterly drove in more than the usual number of overnighters. If the wind was blowing from the north or north-west, The Lappel did not offer good shelter and visiting smacks would frequently lie close in to the Isle of

Grain shore of the Medway, which could be a congested haven especially if a few barges and one or two schooners were brought up there as well.

Mostly the Essexmen were intent on five-fingering out on the Kentish Flats, although they would try for anything that looked profitable, including dragnetting for mullet in the Swale. The Essex smacks could sometimes be seen dredging culch, old oyster shells which were to be re-laid on Essex river oyster grounds to provide anchorage for the drifting oyster spat (larvae) to cling to and grow. These old shells had first to be rid of worm and needed to be spread over a convenient marsh to dry out before being introduced to the cultivated oyster grounds.

In dredging along the north Sheppey shore ('along the land'), the smacks occasionally brought up in the dredges numbers of living oysters which were survivors of the Alston oyster grounds. This old fishery deserves some attention. In 1799 William Alston of Rochester 'butcher and cow-keeper' bought, with a John Payne, the Manor of Minster. Eight years later Alston sold the Manor except for the fishery rights of the foreshore between Garrison Point and Scrapsgate and the Cheney Rock oyster beds. The business, administered from Cheney Rock House, continued right up to the 1880s. Alston's fleet of dredging smacks was apparently based in the Medway and Swale and their shellfish were carried to the London market by smacks and hoys. The fleet included large craft capable of undertaking the deep-sea dredging in the Channel which included natural beds from Dunkirk and the Varne right down to Jersey. Although the heyday of this oyster and scallop free-for-all was over by the 1890s (Olsen's *The Fisherman's Nautical Almanac* of 1885 lists just one Alston smack at Rochester, the *James* (RR 258)), a small and dwindling Channel scallop fishery persisted up to World War II.

In the 1870s and right up to this century it seems that the Swale was good fishing for whitebait. Netting these shoals of immature herrings and sprats had long been officially proscribed on the Medway, although The Lappel between the western entrance of the Swale and Sheerness was free fishing ground and evidently used by Essex, Gravesend and other Kentish fishermen. According to Dr Murie, Essexmen used to work dragnets for whitebait in June and July all round the Isle of Sheppey. This is confirmed by W.L. and Mrs Wyllie in their book *London to The Nore* published in 1905: 'At Queenborough, bawleys and smacks come from many places to fish for whitebait along the banks of the Swale. If you get up early in the morning you may see the men rowing round the edges of the flats and, after the net is shot, striking the water with their oars to chase the fish to their doom. The whitebait is of no use unless caught in time for the early train. Thus, when ordinary folks think of rising, the nets are all fluttering dry at the mast-heads.' This perhaps sounds more like Mrs Wyllie than the great artist himself and she can be imagined standing in the companionway of their moored barge-yacht *Four Brothers* and enjoying the first warm shafts of sunshine, having cruised down the previous evening from Cockham Wood on an Edwardian summer weekend.

*Ethel* (RR 6), a Medway bawley photographed trawling in the Thames Estuary c.1910. She is leading the trawl in a topsail and one-reef breeze. On board are the brothers Charles 'Gosh' Pocock and Harry 'Masher' Pocock.

## *Milton*

At Milton almost all signs of its more heroic maritime past have now been obliterated. It is true that the handsome timber-framed merchants' houses in the High Street are solid evidence of a prosperous existence for some, but the equally historical district about the head of Milton Creek where most of the fishing families lived has been tragically disfigured by modern industry.

In Elizabethan times Milton had four quays and 26 vessels of between 10 and 20 tons. By the 18th century there are records of colliers and hoys owned by Sittingbourne and Milton traders, and in the 19th century and first half of the present century scores of sailing barges worked out of Milton and Murston on the other side of the creek. But Milton's oyster fishery predates the known history of the port, having been granted by King John in 1205 to the abbot and monks of Faversham.

It was a sizeable fishery at one time. According to Hasted's history of Kent of 1782, the Company of Fishermen or Dredgers then numbered 140 freemen who leased grounds in the Swale from the lord of the manor for £100 and four bushels of oysters annually. These grounds extended eastwards to the boundary with the Faversham oyster fishery and to the west as far as King's Ferry. The nearest point at the Lillies, just off the mouth of Milton Creek, is still known alternatively as 'The Grounds'. Until 1709 Milton men had also dredged in the lower Medway but, after many disputes, articles of agreement were drawn up and signed on 7th May of that year between Thomas Herbert, 'lord of the manor of Middleton, alias Milton' and a number of Rochester fishermen who presumably included the jury of the day. This event, which is still spoken of by Medway fishermen as 'the parting of the ways', settled Milton's claims by allocating to it most of Stangate Creek and The Lappel area just inside the mouth of the Medway.

An old notebook of Richard Prall, former Town Clerk of Rochester, contains the following entry: 'The right of the Milton men to fish on Lapwell (if it can be called a right) is founded on Articles made in 1709 between the Fisheries of Rochester and Milton to which the Corporation of Rochester as Conservators of the River ought to have been party. Lapwell is by that Deed given in exchange for other oyster grounds.'

We have it on the word of Daniel Defoe that at one time Milton oysters were the most famous in Kent, but we know that Milton men went much farther afield than their own grounds. Even today older residents remember stories of previous generations of men who went to the North Sea and Channel Islands in smacks and indeed there are scraps of evidence that in Victoria's reign Milton's fishermen crewed in smacks of up to 30 tons in the deep-sea oyster and scallop fishery, while smaller craft of 5 to 20 tons worked the Kentish Flats as well as the Swale.

Milton's Swale oyster grounds remained in cultivation until the severe frosts of the 1890s practically destroyed the whole stock and, local legend has it, ruined a rich merchant, John Hills. Judging by the number of advertisements of fishing smacks for sale in the local press during late Victorian times it is possible that oyster dredging was in

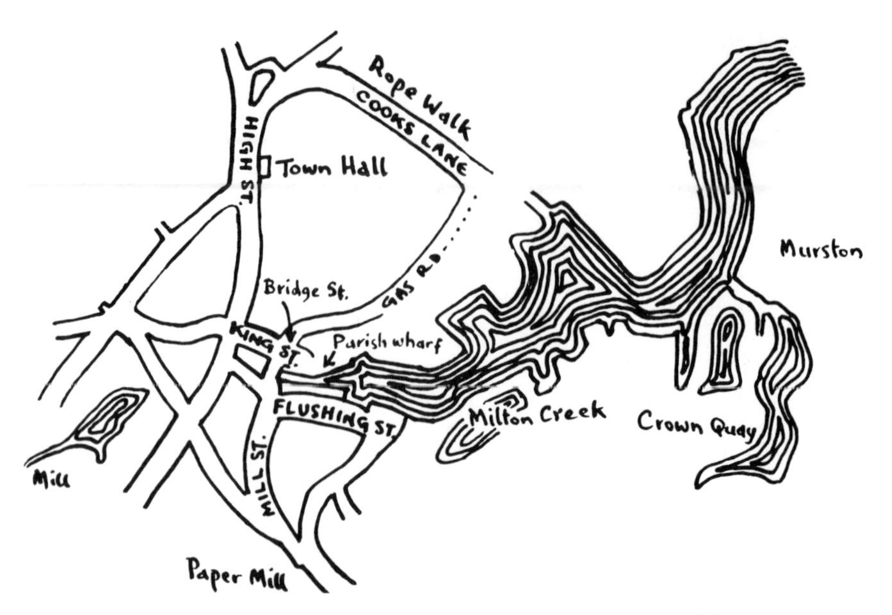


Sketch of old Milton before the fishermen's streets were demolished.

decline anyway as pollution from the paper mills took its toll. However, according to Ted Bingham (as recorded by Alan Cordell and Leslie Williams in *The Past Glory of Milton Creek*), when he was a boy in the 1880s there was still a good fleet of bawleys and these were employed on, apart from oyster dredging, spratting and five-fingering, the fishermen selling this catch for fertiliser at 6d (2½p) a bushel. At this time the barge-building yards on Milton Creek still constructed smaller craft as well. Generations of the Taylor family built and repaired fishing boats up to about 1915 and, although they finished somewhat earlier, Mantle's and Shrubsall's yards are also known to have built fishing craft from the 1860s onwards, again as shown by the local newspapers of the period.

Although the main oyster grounds in the Swale were not apparently worked systematically after the 1890s the Stangate Creek part of the fishery continued to be actively exploited by the Stangate Oyster Fisheries Co. at least until the 1920s. Some local men still worked there as employees under the foreman, Mr W.G.N. Fox, and a number of Rochester-registered fishing boats were in use on these grounds. This business continued in the hands of lessees until about 1940, and the walls of an old brick building said to have been connected with it could still be seen as a picturesque ruin on Chetney until the late 1960s.

As usual with oyster ground rights, the boundaries were a source of trouble. Rochester's Oyster and Floating Fishery claimed the right to dredge at the mouth of Stangate Creek north of an imaginary diagonal line drawn from the entrance to Sharfleet Creek to Deadman's Island on the east side of the mouth of Stangate, but this was hotly contested by the lessees. One ploy some Medway fishermen tried was to throw out their dredges within the disputed triangle but not actually lift them until their bawley had drifted well outside the Stangate Creek entrance. In 1924 one Strood boat with a crew of three men dredged 10,000 oysters from that part of Stangate so it is not surprising that the dredging rights were a contentious matter.

The last full-time Milton fishermen (and freemen of the fishery) were the two brothers Redshaw (usually known in the town as 'Redshall') and their father Ben who had a wet fish shop and curing shed in New Road. They were frequently to be seen with a couple of sacks of winkles slung on an old bicycle, having leased cockle and winkle beds off Elmley Island in the Swale and also worked Stangate Creek by picking up sundry shellfish there. Later on, in the 1950s, the Redshaw brothers, Tom and Harry, graduated to motorbike and sidecar for carrying their shellfish. The old fishing families still lived at that time in the lower part of the town, now almost completely swept away, mainly in Flushing Street, Bridge street and King Street (where the creek reached right up to the back gardens and in former times fishermen's skiffs could be brought in on a high tide right up to their own landing steps).

Although fishing had almost finished as a full-time job by the 1900s, traditions died hard and a number of men fished in their spare time or when laid-off from their usual jobs. In the 1930s there were half a dozen boats of varied provenance kept at the top of the creek for this purpose. The men used the old fishermen's hard which was between the Parish Wharf and Prentis' Quay (just below on the Milton side). The boats were moored on a drying mudbank nearby known as The Duckle. Jim Green recalled that his father and others used to hang their nets to dry along the fence behind Eastwood's warehouse. The creek did not finish at the Parish Wharf even in those days but turned westwards for some distance to meet the outflow from the Periwinkle stream.

Old barges' boats could be picked up cheaply at this time. Jim Green bought his first, complete with standing lugsail for 30/- (£1.50); these were heavy but shapely clinker boats and excellent for fluing for flatfish. The corked and weighted standing net, anchored at each end, was shot across a rillway or creek, then the man working the net stood in the stern of the boat and shook the 'ruggles' (sometimes called 'jingles'), a collection of iron rings on a rope, to make a noise under the water and drive the fish to the net. One end was usually anchored in the shallows but as the whole net was in water only a few feet deep it had plenty of slack bellying to the young flood questing up the rills.

Flue nets were gathered vertically through the mesh at both ends by a 'broach line' stretching between the cork line and lead line (thus the 'broaching' or sometimes 'britching'); this tended to trap fish that had managed to work their way along the net.

Windmill Creek on Sheppey was a favourite spot for flounders and it was a good place to catch them by griping. After a call at the 'Harty Inn' on a Saturday evening in autumn a party of four or five young men could reckon to get between 100 and 150 fish by this time-hallowed-method. They worked down the rillways as the tide receded and feeling with both hands in the muddy water, clouded the water deliberately so

'Bluey' Brown and his son on their boat *Emu* at Prentis Quay, Milton Creek in the early 1930s. The old warehouse of the brickmakers and barge owners, Eastwoods, is in the background.
(J. Green)

that the fish did not see the approaching man. On touching a fish the trick was to immediately press down on it and grab with both hands, trying to avoid the sharp spike on its side, and having got a firm grip finally to drop it into the waiting sack.

Milton men were also adept at the other ancient fishing technique of creek-stopping: setting fish weirs across the local rillways. A number of posts were driven into the bed of the creek and a length of old net lashed to the posts and, having been weighted along the bottom, put down into the mud. The fish, mainly flounders again, were caught because they came up the creeks as the tide made, either swimming over the net or past it in the shallows at each end; when the tide fell and they attempted to get back to the main channels the way was blocked by the stop-nets. Hoop-nets were used too, the hinged variety which shut like a purse when hauled up. Baited on the cords strung across the middle of the hoop, they were suspended from a boat on a warp which divided into bridles made fast to both sides of the hoop so that it could quickly snap shut when jerked and hauled every few minutes to the surface.

For fishing purposes barges' boats needed to be fitted with a wash-strake to give more freeboard, but larger boats of any suitable type were liable to appear in Milton Creek and Jim Green later had a Hastings lugger with a lute stern called *Curlew*. She had a hot-bulb Kelvin engine which had to be started with a blowlamp. Model T Ford engines were preferred as soon as the men could afford them and an early marine conversion kit could be obtained. Ernest 'Desker' Green (Jim's father) bought the first boat locally to have a motor, a single cylinder paraffin engine in an ex-Admiralty cutter, which he purchased from Dickie Evenden, the Kingsferry Bridge barge huffler.

It is characteristic of those economical times that the boat was named *Otter* by the simple means of removing the first brass letter of the word 'cutter' and changing the next. 'Pickle' Coomber had *Shamrock* and another *Shamrock* was owned by 'Burglar' Spice. 'Pipe' Marsh had *Scotchman* and Tom Green had *Meg* and *Sez You*. Other local fishing men of the 1920s remembered by Ernie Pearce were 'Chicken' Capelin and 'Ratty' Stubberfield: Milton was as fond of its nicknames as any other fishing community of that era. Other familiar figures were the luters employed by the town council to keep the main creek from silting up. The last two to hold this job were Dick Gregory and Jim Hatton. They stood in thigh boots in the creek as the tide fell working the black silt with wooden pushers so that it washed away downtide, helped by the opening of floodgates at the head of the creek.

In those days the fishermen still sold their catch door-to-door around the town. A string of flounders or dabs weighing about 3lb sold for 1/- (5p), rising to about 2/6 (12½p) in the 1930s. Winkles fetched 6d a quart and mussels 6d a gallon, both sold uncooked. Picking up shellfish was a natural way of either earning a few shillings or providing a free meal for the family, with cockles and winkles plentiful at various places along the Swale. One man, Charlie 'Pipe' Marsh, suffered an unpleasant death while out winkling on the mudflats. Fog came down and he apparently lost his sense of direction and was engulfed by the silently rising tide.

Milton men fluing for flatfish in Windmill Creek, Isle of Sheppey in the 1930s. Tom Green is hauling in the flue net and Ernest Green pulls ahead with the oars to maintain tension on the net as it comes in over the stern. (J. Green)

The Essex bawleymen came over for Sheppey cockles, dropping hook off Minster, Leysdown or even on the Horse Sand in the Swale to wait for the tide to recede so that they could jump down on the sands and start raking. Their stranded craft were a common sight heeled over on these cockle grounds until well after World War II. The men worked quickly while the tide was out, raking out the cockles and filling bushel baskets which they carried back to their bawley suspended from shoulder yokes to be checked in by the skipper. Mostly the cocklers used short rakes and separate lave nets, hand nets on a stirrup-shaped iron frame, but I was told that some used a 'dygal', a rake and net combined (the name probably a corruption of dydle, if this is the correct spelling of the old word for hand net). Arthur Croucher remembers seeing the Essexmen sitting around on deck while they waited for the tide to ebb and playing cards – gambling with their day's wages before the work had even begun.

Bert Stroud of Whitstable owned three fishing boats at one time and Arthur worked for a while on these in the 1950s, shrimping and fishing for herring and sprats according to the season. One of the boats was the Stroud family's old smack *Gamecock* which was then purely a motor fishing boat. One day they were working the other side of the Estuary in the Barrow Deep when they came upon a lone cat swimming for its life far from the land. The fishermen thought it had probably been tossed from a homeward bound ship as the problems of quarantine began to loom. The cat, an almost invisible speck in that vast expanse of water, was fortunate to be seen by the Kentishmen who plucked it from the sea and quietly took it home.

Eeling was a popular activity in summer and a number of different techniques came into play according to the fishermen's inclination. Eel traps, long and tubular and made of wire mesh in recent times, were put down with marker buoys in deep water, and of course shallow creeks were the place to go sapping (dangling balls of worms threaded on hemp

An engraving from *The Penny Magazine* of 1837 vintage of Kentish Oyster smacks. The two men in a small boat in the foreground seem to be working a dredge under oars.

or worsted). 'Patsy' Hudson was noted for taking the whole of his large family on sapping trips in an old boat. South Deeps and Captain's Creek were favourite places for sapping on the south side of the Swale; it was most successful when done on a rising tide in no more than about three feet depth of water.

Jim Green described how his father had used one of the traditional three pronged eel shears in a brackish pond called Cornford's Lake (which may once have been a duck decoy). He could not see his quarry but simply worked round the water's edge lifting the eight foot shaft and letting it slide down through his hands into the mud bottom of the pool. Others had their favourite marshy places where the eels could be found in the fleets, often in small holes in the clay banks where the shears were thrust blindly, and sometimes caught a writhing eel between its tines.

## *Conyer*

This is perhaps the place to remember the small oyster fishery once owned by the manor of Teynham and, in more recent times, by the Conyer Oyster Company, a commercial enterprise working out of Conyer Creek in the early years of this century. Don Sattin's book *Just off the Swale* notes that there were oyster grounds on both sides of Fowley Island and oyster pits on the island itself. There was even a steam launch to tow the men to the grounds in their skiffs but, like Milton, there is hardly a trace of this activity now. Don Sattin says that the oyster company once owned *Bessie*, an old bawley, which in summer went trawling for soles between South Deep and the mouth of Faversham Creek.

# 6

# *Faversham*

Faversham's oyster fishery is believed to have existed since the 12th century and lays claim to being the oldest recorded company in the world. In 1205 King John endowed the abbot and monks of Faversham with the local oyster beds and common fishery, to which he added the oyster fishery at Milton. The abbey was suppressed in 1538 but in 1630 Charles I gave the manor of Faversham to Sir Dudley Digges and for many generations the company of free dredgers collectively paid a rent of £1.3s.4d annually to the lord of the manor whose steward supervised the fishery. The boundaries were indicated in 1591 after an inquiry by Sir Thomas Fludd and others, and in 1609 a more detailed survey was made by Sir Michael Sands and other eminent persons of the time. The boundaries then described were repeated in the fishery's first Act of Parliament in 1788 which recognised the benefits of exporting oysters to 'Foreign Parts' and referred to the fishery as 'a Nursery of Seamen for the Royal Navy'.

Daniel Defoe had written of the Dutch hoys and luggers loading oysters at Faversham in the 1720s; and Edward Jacob's *History of Faversham* in 1774 noted that 110 families were then principally supported by the fishery. Jacob says that some 11,000 bushels of oysters worth over £3,000 were exported yearly to Holland and Flanders (although some of this total may have been supplied by adjoining fisheries). To augment the spatfall on the North Kent grounds even at that time oyster brood was shipped in from Land's End, Scotland and France.

The Act of 1788 refers to the usual problem with the North Kent oyster fisheries of poaching by neighbours, despite the then well defined boundaries. It rehearses the actions which might be taken to bring the offenders before the County Quarter Sessions. The fishery itself then held two courts annually under the lord of the manor's steward, the Admiralty Court at Easter for appointing a foreman, treasurer and four members of the jury for the ensuing year, and the Water Court in July to open the grounds. A water bailiff was also appointed to maintain the beacons marking the grounds and was entitled to collect a few pence from members of the fishery for 'beaconage'.

An Act of 1840 gave further statutory blessing to the Faversham Oyster Fishery Company, repeating in minute detail the boundaries

Front Brents, Faversham c.1900. This row of cottages facing the creek still exists but the interiors are no doubt very different from the days when they were the homes of fishermen and bargemen at the turn of the century. (A.E. Jemmett)

from 'Teynham Robbs' in the west to beyond Shellness on the tip of Sheppey and out to the Columbine to the east (where the Seasalter and Ham oyster fishery grounds began), specified the date of the annual Water Court and the rules for the election of the foreman, treasurer, secretary and twelve jury members from among the freemen.

Although the fishery possessed 14 miles of some of the finest oyster grounds in the country it went through a financial crisis again in 1887 when a petition was presented in Chancery for its winding-up. However the company survived and in 1930 a further Act permitted the 'Company or Fraternity of Free Fishermen and Dredgermen of the Manor and Hundred of Faversham' to be dissolved and its assets transferred to the Faversham Oyster Fishery Company, a limited liability company with a share capital which was thought to be more suited to modern conditions than the relic of the medieval guild system which it replaced. The first meeting of the new company's directors was held in August 1930.

By this time the fishery had leased part of its grounds to the Seasalter and Ham Oyster Fishery Company of Whitstable (who had acquired title to the ancient Seasalter fishery back in 1895), and the number of men getting even part-time employment from the Faversham grounds had greatly declined. From 1903 the fishery's oysters were no longer sold direct to the public due to the effects of pollution from the town's sewers. After prolonged litigation a meagre amount of compensation was paid by the town corporation as damages and shared among the

A scene on the Town Quay at Faversham c.1908. The fisherman appears to be unloading sprats straight from a drift net which he has probably been using from his boat in the Swale.
(A.E. Jemmett)

fishermen and surviving widows. After 1903 oysters dredged would have had to be sold to merchants or the Whitstable companies for relaying on their unpolluted grounds or in purification tanks.

As some indication of the fishery's importance in better times, an old register shows 136 names of men admitted as freemen between 1834 and 1901. Only the eldest sons of existing freemen had the right to be apprenticed, and to obtain his freedom of the fishery a young man had to serve his seven years and have found a wife. The last apprenticed was Bert Jemmett in 1929 at the age of 13 years and in that decade there were still about 50 or 60 freemen to attend the annual Water Court and some 20 apprentices.

The Faversham Oyster Fishery's Jury Book for the period 1918-1924 shows the weekly earnings against each bawley or smack. The jury set the men's pay which usually ranged between 5/- (25p) and 14/- (70p) for each 100 oysters dredged, so earnings for each boat came out at something between about £5 to £10 and, very exceptionally, approaching £20, this sum having to be shared by up to four men in the crew and a share for the boat. The maximum number of oysters to be dredged by each man in the week – his stint – and the price per 100 oysters, was fixed every few weeks by the jury, according to the quantities wanted by the merchants, who were either the Whitstable companies or George Tabor Ltd of Billingsgate.

The maximum stint in the period was no more than 1,000 full-sized oysters per man per week, but it was sometimes as low as 250. Up to 1920 it was not unusual for the fishery to sell 20,000 oysters a week and in the December of that year the total reached 34,000 which gave the *Alma*'s crew a record total pay of £19.12s for 4,900 oysters dredged, a handy Christmas bonus. During these years the Faversham fishery was still laying young oysters (brood) as necessary to replenish its grounds and leasing parts of them for merchants' own use as well. The decline started in 1921 when the mysterious 'oyster mortality', which was causing such alarm at neighbouring Whitstable, killed about half of the oyster stock on the Faversham grounds.

No doubt for a while the relative scarcity of supply put up prices, for in 1924 when the Jury book ends, it is recorded that George Tabor was offering 18/- (90p) a 100, the Faversham company paying its members 15/- (75p), to be dredged in stints of 400 per man in a five day week.

The number of working boats gradually declined from a dozen at the end of World War I to about half that number by 1924. The Jury Book shows that in early 1918 the craft employed in dredging were the bawleys *Emma, Elizabeth, Lydia, Mary Ann* and *Secret*; the smacks *Alfred, Alma, Annie, Diadem* and *Isabella*; and the *Ellen* and *Hero* which are not now remembered with any certainty. In May 1924 only *Alma, Annie, Alfred, Elizabeth, Mary Ann* and *Secret* were still enaged in regular oyster dredging, although some of the others could have still been at work fishing and dredging on the Kentish Flats.

Typical of the older and smaller clinker-built bawleys was *Lydia* registered as FM 19 (the initials FM and the single F were both used for boats on the Faversham register). She was registered in 1879 in the ownership of William Thompsett of Milton and described as a yawl. On being sold to Ben Jemmett in 1894 the register lists her as a 'borley'. She was shown as 28ft on the keel, 29.1ft in length, with a beam of 9.6ft and tonnage of 7.22. She remained in the family's ownership until about 1930. The Jemmetts also had the venerable bawley *Lass of Kent* (FM 155) until she was broken up in 1932; one of several fishing boats of this name along the Kent coast, she was 31.7ft in length with a beam of 12ft. Other craft remembered well include the smack *Alma* (FM 101), owned by Isaac 'Ike' Dane, a fast boat in the impromptu races home in the Swale; the bawley *William* (FM 317) of 25.6ft by 9ft, owned by William G. Dane before 1900 and by Alfred Gregory up to the 1920s; and the Gregory family's 36ft by 12ft *Secret* (FM 23), whose hulked bones lay opposite Hollowshore where the Faversham and Oare Creeks meet (always known as 'Hollyshore' to Faversham folk).

Jim Gregory's little *Emma* (FM 22) remains at Faversham and is used for trawling still. She is thought to have started life as a Leigh cockle-boat around 1860, was brought to Faversham around the turn of the century and doubled over her original clinker strakes at Conyer Creek in 1916. Her dimensions are, length 23.4ft, keel length 22ft, beam 9ft, hold depth 2.3ft (tonnage 4.80). The *Emma* was bought by Jim Gregory's father, Frank 'Turp' Gregory, in 1930 and was used in the oyster fishery right up to its end in about 1948. The *Emma* had a Bollinder engine installed in the 1930s but, apart from her, only *Fiona* and *Jessie* of the privately owned craft had engines. The fishery's ex-Lowestoft smack

The little ex-Milton bawley *Lydia* (FM 19) at the top of Faversham Creek c.1900. She was bought from William Thomsett of Milton by Ben Jemmett Senr. around 1894 to be skippered by Walter Jemmett, one of his sons. (A.E. Jemmett)

*Shield* was also powered with a 9hp petrol/paraffin Kelvin but the men did not fully trust it and had a cut-down sail rigged in case of mechanical failure. The fishery's other vessel was a watchboat, *Edith,* moored close to Harty Ferry until 1939, mainly to ensure that the yachtsmen did not disturb the oyster grounds. During the last few years of the oyster fishery the remaining families took it in turns to work a week at a time and this came round about one week in four.

The Jemmetts' *Mary Ann* (FM 144) was still fully rigged and unpowered when sold away to a Medway buyer in 1938, by which time the Leighmen and other neighbouring fishermen generally had motors and could get some sort of living even in a flat calm from five-fingering if not fishing, while the Faversham men mostly had to have an unproductive day if they could not find enough wind. The *Mary Ann* was a large bawley of 40ft by 12ft, bought from Queenborough in about 1904 with a mizzen mast fitted. This was removed by Alfred 'Dunner' Jemmett who then had her mainmast moved aft a little to maintain sail balance. The mainsail was set loose-footed to a boom, as was the Faversham bawleymen's style, and she had the usual jib-headed topsail with the luff held to the topmast by a jackline. She, like *Emma,* was doubled by a yard at Conyer, for £10. *Mary Ann* leaked at first when this was done but then took up and remained tight afterwards. Also her rails were lowered by the Jemmett family to ease the work of hauling dredges.

One of the tasks *Mary Ann* performed to earn her keep was to fetch culch from Leigh-on-Sea for the oyster merchant, George Tabor, to lay on his leased grounds thus providing anchorage for new oyster spat. The material in this case was cockle shells – which Leigh Creek still has in abundance – and some 400 bushels were loaded, lowering *Mary Ann*'s waterline almost to deck level. To find enough water in the creek this had to be done on good spring tides. It was a summer evening job, after the normal day's work was done, the bawley being sailed over to Leigh sometimes three times in a week when weather and tides were favourable. The crew often had first to shovel the shells from the creek's edge into their skiff and then fill baskets for hoisting aboard the bawley, finally tipping the load into the hold between bulkhead compartments. To finish off, sacks of shells were laid along the decks as well.

Apart from being hard work, the job was smelly, a pervasive odour clinging to these cockle shells. Once, Bert got permission to take a break and stroll along to Southend to watch a carnival procession. The streets were crowded but Bert soon noticed that folk were politely standing back to give him plenty of space.

The culching trips often ended with *Mary Ann* sailing home to Faversham in the dark with the aid of a compass complete with oil lamp alongside in a fitted box, the whole lashed to eyebolts on the deck: the fisherman's binnacle.

Bert Jemmett recalled that his grandfather, Ben Jemmett, owned four or five fishing boats but did not 'go away' after the age of 40, leaving his sons to do the fishing; although they were not paid more than pocket-money until they were married and freemen of the fishery.

The Faversham bawley *Mary Ann* (FM 114) with a pleasure party aboard in the 1930s. The wind is light and a large foresail and jib have been set as well as the well patched topsail.

(A.E. Jemmett)

His grandmother could braid nets and make dredge rigging; as in other fishing communities in Victorian times, netting was regarded as women's work.

Three of Ben Jemmett's sons, Alfred 'Dunner', George 'Smiggy' and Walter 'Chasey' Jemmett, bought an ex-Colchester smack, *Edith*, for £90, which they nicknamed 'the waggon' because of her ponderous movements under sail. Finding there was a full set of stowboating gear on board they gave spratting a try, successfully it seems because they came home heavily laden with decks awash.

The normal winter work however was oyster dredging or five-fingering, while summer brought trawling, from the Horse Sand at the eastern end of the Swale down to the Reculver. The usual catch was Dover soles, roker (skate*), plaice and dabs. The wide Estuary was close at hand but the Swale could be productive at times. Howard Dane remembered an occasion on *Alma* in the 1930s having upwards of fifty roker in one haul up the Swale from the Horse Sand. Brown shrimps also came right into Faversham Creek as far as Hollowshore in February. In fact 'Turp' Gregory rarely had to go farther afield than Windmill Creek or the Horse Sand for his shrimps. He would also try for lobsters with the trawl, in 'the Hole' in South Deep. Faversham fishermen had their own jingle about the annual appearance of soles: 'when the corn is in ear the soles will appear.'

Trawl warps were hauled by hand capstans; the Faversham boats did not have the wink posts of the Thames and Medway bawleys. Since the bawleys as well as the smacks at Faversham all had boomed mainsails, brailing was not possible and to reduce mainsail area when trawling the smacksmen's techniques of tricing up the tack and rucking the peak were employed.

Mostly the craft were sailed from moorings in the 'Sump', just below Hollowshore on the other side of the creek but if loaded with hauls of fish or five-fingers they were if at all possible sailed up to the town quays by the tortuous and narrow creek and berthed along the marshy Front Brents. That meant smart sailing indeed, the boats wending quickly and accurately and rarely touching mud. The men were hard about giving way to each other on those occasions although, like other close fishing communities, they helped readily enough in real trouble.

To get to and from the moorings near the mouth of the creek the men followed paths which are still known as 'Drudgermen's Walks'. Many times a young man would be ordered to knock up his skipper at one or two o'clock in the morning and they would find their way by those old familiar creekside tracks to the waiting smack in order to save the ebb out into the Swale.

Five-fingering was a regular occupation, when the wind served, to fill those days when there was not enough oyster dredging work to be done. The same sized dredges were used but so thick were the starfish on the Kentish Flats that quite a small area could yield a full load of about 12

* More precisely, thornback ray.

Another party aboard *Mary Ann* c.1936. There is more of a breeze on this occasion because a smaller foresail and jib are set and the topmast is lowered. The three ports in the bulwarks used for 'shading' out the unwanted debris when oyster dredging are open in this photograph.
(A.E. Jemmett)

Faversham craft in the Swale in the 1920s. The bawley with the stump topmast in the background is probably *William* (FM 317). Neither has an engine and the crews are having to row to make any progress in a near calm. (A.E. Jemmett)

tons. Dredges filled with five-fingers were lighter to haul than oysters but it was still heavy work heaving them up over the boat's rail. It took one tide to get a full load aboard and the same to unload, after the smack arrived at her destination – often under oars if it was feeling the way up a creek in the dark – be it Town Quay, Oare, Conyer Creek, Otterham Quay, or wherever the farmer wanted his fertiliser delivered.

One Christmas Eve *Mary Ann* was sailed by Alfred and Charles 'Gyber' Jemmett up the Medway and into Lower Halstow, only to find that the Newington farmer had not arranged for the horses and tumbrils to be at the quay. That meant walking home to Faversham and then walking back on Boxing Day when, in those days, everyone was at work again. Earnings from selling five-fingers were as low as 12/- (60p) a ton in the 1920s.

Starfish were attracted to cockle 'trails' so they could be found in quantities off Sheppey all the way down from the Cant, past the Spile, Four Fathoms Channel and the Spaniard to Whitstable. At an inquiry held at Tollesbury in 1923 before the Inspector of the Board of Agriculture and Fisheries into an application by the Seasalter & Ham Oyster Fishery Company to appropriate part of the Flats for their exclusive use, it was stated that more than fifty Tollesbury smacks dredged up to 500 tons of five-fingers in a week and sold them to Essex farmers at £1 a ton upwards. Later the House of Commons threw out a private bill by the oyster company designed to give them exclusive rights over 730 acres of the Flats, on the grounds that this area gave employment to some 200 smacksmen for several months of the year.

A Faversham smack probably photographed on the same day. Two men are rowing; the man at the tiller is also working the starboard oar while another crew member goes forward to adjust the headsails. (A.E. Jemmett)

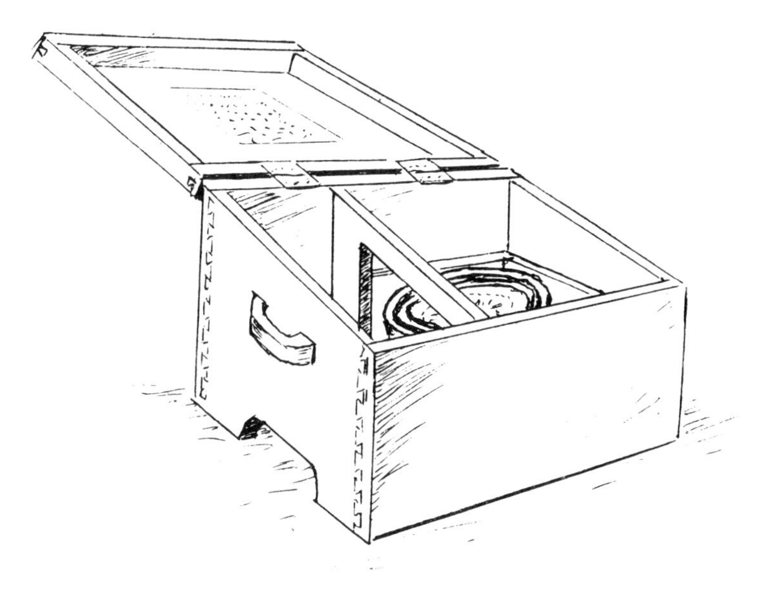

These wooden compass boxes were commonly used on smacks and bawleys. At night they were taken on deck and lashed to an eye or cleat and an oil lamp put in alongside the compass to light it. Sketch by Leslie H. Hill.

Harold Rowden reckoned that the 'Favvies' were the best dredgermen, followed by his fellow Whitstable smacksmen, with the Essexmen trailing in third place, although this may be accounted for by the traditional rivalry between Essexmen and the Kentish men. At any rate the Faversham men had evidently mastered the art of rucking their vessels' mainsails to produce a very slow dredging speed. 'They could pick up a hairpin.' The admiration did not seem to be returned. Faversham folk were a closely-knit community frequently addressing each other as 'neighbour' and they did not think Whitstable people very friendly. One fisherman said 'They want five bob to take hold of a rope there.' On the other hand the Whitstable whelkers would pay one shilling's reward for the return of any pots they had lost and Faversham men were pleased to take this modest bounty for the pots they sometimes trawled up. It was noted that each family engaged in whelking could identify their own pots.

Faversham fishermen had their own informal market place for selling from barrows straight to the housewives. It was at the approach to the old iron swingbridge across the head of the creek where the railings surrounding the parish pump were useful for the fishermen or their wives to display strings of fish for sale. Some, including Bert Jemmett's grandmother, also had a stall at Faversham's Guildhall market where deals could be struck with local fish merchants as well as the passing townsfolk.

For any minor maintenance work on the fishing boats' hulls the Faversham men used 'Hills's Hard', a shingle bank just below their moorings near the mouth of the creek on the Oare side. To scrub off, clean and tar one side of the boat before the tide returned was a race against time. It meant the usual burning off and drying operation by flaming the surface with paraffin-soaked rags and the final tarring as the tide crept in around the men's feet.

The last sails came from Whitstable mostly (in 1937 Goldfinch's could supply a bawley's mainsail for £25) but earlier there had been a local sailmaker working in the old timber-framed building just below the swingbridge. His name was Alf Lott and he was equally capable of making a barge's sails as a set for a small boat. On the other side of the creek remain some of the terraced cottages of Front Brents, originally the homes of a number of fishing families.

Another reminder of old times is Smack Alley which runs from Abbey Street towards the creek: a pub of that name once stood there. Immediately opposite across Abbey Street is the Phoenix Tavern, thought to incorporate an ancient building used as a hostel by the monks of Faversham Abbey which, from soon after its founding by King Stephen in 1147 until its suppression by Henry VIII, owned the Faversham fishery. But, to bring the story back within living memory, close by there was until quite recently Keiller's jam factory, whose well known white-glazed pottery jars were used almost universally by the crews of the last Faversham smacks and bawleys as their tea mugs.

# 7

# *Whitstable*

The ancient association of the Whitstable area and its native oysters is well known, with documentary evidence that the Romans appreciated the fine quality of this Kentish shellfish. Oyster cultivation was evidently organised through the guild system in medieval times when the Company of Free Dredgers enjoyed the exclusive right to dredge and fish under licence from the lord of the manor. As early as 1489 a court at Canterbury ruled that there should be no dredging during the spawning season of 1st May to 1st August. By the 18th century it is recorded that the lord of the manor received an annual royalty of £1 for each dredging boat and 2/- (10p) from each dredgerman; but in 1792 the marine portion of the manor was sold to Thomas Foord who then conveyed it to the Company, and the following year they became incorporated by an Act of Parliament under the title of the Company of Free Fishers and Dredgers of Whitstable. By a charter of George III the Company was given the exclusive right to call the local oysters 'Royal Natives'. The annual Water Court previously held by the lord of the manor became the responsibility of the Company itself which elected its own foreman, jurymen and other officers to run the fishery. At this time the practice of allowing the sons of non-freemen to become free dredgers after a seven years' apprenticeship was stopped and only the sons of existing members were admitted.

By 1881 a rapid growth in the number of freemen led to the rules being changed again and only the eldest sons of freemen were enrolled for apprenticeship at the age of fourteen. By this time there were 508 members on the Company's books and after about ten years of difficult trading it was nearly £30,000 in debt. A number of freemen could not be given employment but still received one-third pay; widows and sick freemen were also being provided for in the Company's welfare net. 1881 was a better year however with about four million French oysters laid and good sales made so that the debt was reduced. I have this information from contemporary accounts lent to me by Harold Rowden.* These notes also record that the following year some Whitstable boats were sent up to work the Essex grounds and bring back oyster brood, for which the men were paid between 1/6 and 3/6 (17½p) a hundred. As a general comment on earnings during this period, J.T. Reeves observed 'In 1865 the Pay was £65 and up to 1880 never

* Compiled by I. Reeves (1788-1873), J.T. Reeves (b.1845) and J. Seales.

An engraving from *The Illustrated London News* of 1883 showing the busy scene at Whitstable in the oyster fishery's heyday. Note the typical small pole-masted smack of the period on which four men are hauling dredges. Below men are landing oysters with the large fleet of oyster smacks offshore.

Whitstable oystermen landing from their skiff and bringing oysters to the store in net bags holding the old measure of a wash. This photograph dates from before the First World War.
(Douglas West Studios)

exceeded that ... No spat or Brood on either the Ground or the flats for 20 years. Oysters everywhere very scarce. The company paying £9 to £10 per Bushell for half ware and brood from Essex ...' This scarcity was of course reflected in sale prices. Mr Reeves noted 'In one year, I think 1863, over £100,000 of oysters were sold in London Market and (from the) Shore the price being £5 per Bushell. The price of Oyster Natives was then increased and in 1878 they realized £12.'

By 1890 the company had its own salesman at 26 Fish Street Hill, Billingsgate but the debts had risen to nearly £50,000 and the severe winter killed much of the oyster stock on the grounds. More bad winters including the great frost of 1895 took further toll of the fishery, and by that time the public health authorities were making well publicised investigations into the connection between typhoid fever and polluted shellfish. The dredgers and their families were consequently in considerable distress, particularly during the winters when charitable gentlefolk organised soup kitchens and distributions of groceries and coal. By 1896 an Act of Parliament was necessary to put the fishery on a proper commercial basis as a limited liability company with a nominal capital of £250,000, about half of which was distributed to the freemen and the balance was available to sell to the public.

Thereafter the affairs of the Company improved gradually with good spatfalls on the grounds and Flats every year from 1897 to 1902. Sales were about £50,000 in 1900, falling to £29,000 in 1902 when there was another 'oyster scare' over typhoid risks. Selling prices were then 16/- a hundred for Royals (selected natives), having previously been 18/- (90p)

Another photograph from the pre-First World War period showing Whitstable smacksmen working their oyster dredges. (Douglas West Studios)

for Royals and double that retail according to A.O. Collard (falling to 14/- (70p) by 1913 although the volume of trade had by then picked up again). According to Collard's book, written in 1901, the Whitstable company distributed between 10 and 15 million oysters annually to home and overseas customers.

To round off this selection from written sources the following quote is from A.O. Collard's book: 'In the Balance-sheet issued under date 31st May, 1901, the value of the stock of oysters, brood, and halfware is put at £64,846, being the amount actually paid for it by the Company, and does not include the enormous value of the spat which has been deposited by nature on the Company's ground during the last four years. The Company is managed by a Board of five directors, with a secretary, who also fills the old office of treasurer, as he receives the money and pays the men – a storesman, who superintends the working staff in the oyster depot; a foreman, who controls the working of the fleet; and a water-bailiff, whose duty it is to collect the anchorage and other dues payable to the Company, and who carries as a badge of office a small blue oar. The old office of bellman is abolished, as the foreman himself communicates the orders for the day's work or 'stint' by calling them out from the office steps. The members of the Company no longer take apprentices, and the supply of men is kept up from among the shareholders, and from flatsmen if the supply is short, preference being given to those flatsmen who have been shareholders, but have sold their shares. The Company at present employs about 120 men, though there are 300 dredgers and flatsmen engaged altogether at Whitstable in 80 smacks, each of which has a name and number.' He also noted that when the Company bought oysters dredged from outside their grounds they paid the flatsmen 7/- (35p) for a wash (about 5¼ gallons).

The oyster grounds at the mouth of the East Swale were divided in a patchwork fashion. The Whitstable Oyster Company's grounds (known as 'the Shore') were bordered to the north by the last stretch of the Faversham Oyster Company's grounds and to the west by the Pollard grounds of the Seasalter & Ham Oyster Fishery Company Ltd, whose other triangular shaped area was the Ham grounds beyond the Columbine, northwards again. The Whitstable Oyster Company's grounds were fenced with stakes and marked off in squares by swinging beacons for working purposes. The Company had three watchboats within memory; these old smacks were *Native* (F 101), *Betsy* (F 229) and *Thomas Foord* (F 99), the first anchored at the Bay Buoy and the others on the northern boundary. These craft were mostly too old for work, although the *Thomas Foord* was at times pressed into service if the day's stint for the Company required an additional dredging boat. The Seasalter & Ham Company owned several smacks including the old *Czarina* (F 131), *Blackball* (F 129) (a boomsail bawley), *Nellie* (F 79) and *Three Brothers* (F 134). The *Nellie* was at one time used as a watchboat on the Pollard grounds, replaced in 1928 by *Stormy Petrel* (F 71) skippered by Bert 'Ponger' Stroud. *Three Brothers* was a watchboat on the Ham grounds, the crew earning an extra 1/- (5p) a night for this work. The men on these watchboats worked alternate weekends afloat keeping a look-out for poachers. They had Fridays ashore in lieu of the weekend and, as Company employees, were paid a daily wage of 15/- (75p), whereas the Whitstable Oyster Company men, as shareholders, were generally paid by the stint of oysters required and dredged, although they would have received extra pay for their watching.

The Whitstable Oyster Company's stock carrier was the smack *Postboy* (F 37) and the Seasalter and Ham's largest smack, *Seasalter* (F 322), was their carrier. She was skippered by Albert 'Skipper' Stroud from late 1919 until December 1924, by which time the bulk of the Whitstable fleet of smacks and bawleys were fast disappearing, mostly sold away in the hard times caused by the severe occurrence of oyster disease in 1923/24.

The *Favourite* (F 69), now high and dry on the beach at Whitstable was, like *Postboy* and *Seasalter*, employed in carrying oyster brood (immature stock) from Essex at one time. Other craft owned by the companies were *Sydney Brown* (F 163), an old ketch yacht worked by the Whitstable company, and *Marmion* (F 126), a powered ketch of 43.4ft built by Anderson, Rigden & Perkins just after World War I. Her first owners were George Tabor's of Billingsgate and she was worked on their leased grounds, skippered at one time by Harold Rowden's father, Jesse. Although rigged for sailing she had twin Gleniffer engines that did most of the work; she had a very wide counter stern from which five men could work with a dredge apiece. Harold believed that the boatyard had laid down a keel for a barge but with timber then in short supply they did not have enough to continue so they built *Marmion* instead. This

Hauling dredges on the smack *XL* (F 61) owned by Harry Goldsmith who is aboard. The foresail is hauled to windward and the mainsail eased off so that the smack is laid-to. There are two smacks behind, one being *Herbert* (F 97). (Brian Hadler)

Oyster dredging in progress on three Whitstable smacks, probably in the early 1920s. The nearest smack is *Invicta* (F 58). (Douglas West Studios)

ketch was sold away to the Sunderland Pilotage Authority in 1943. The other big ketch that was a familiar sight off Whitstable until the last few years of oyster cultivation there was *Speedwell*, an unusual craft for this work, having a length of around 50ft with a clipper bow and short bowsprit at one end and a counter stern at the other. She was built at Burnham-on-Crouch as a motor-dredger in 1908 and was decked over at Whitstable where she was owned by the Seasalter and Ham Company from 1920 until 1967. During this time she was ketch rigged with a stump topmast. She had a Kelvin type 44 diesel engine but still set some sail for dredging hove-to downtide.

In the period between 1900 and the outbreak of World War I there were upwards of seventy smacks at work at Whitstable, the majority Whitstable built but with some Essex smacks and Medway bawleys (all boom rigged) amongst them. Earlier, in the mid-19th century, there were (according to the *Kentish Gazette* of 1853) '100 yawls or dredging boats, the estimated value of which is about £10,000'. It is clear from old prints that these were mainly clinker craft of 25 to 30ft in length, with pole-masted cutter rig. The word yawl has relatively recently acquired a precise meaning in terms of sail rig but originally was used to describe a small double-ended boat in the Norsemen's style (cf. yol in Scandinavia and yole in the Orkneys and Shetlands). Later the term was applied to other types of small boats such as the 22ft transomed craft called yawles in Admiralty plans of the early 18th century. In the 19th and early 20th centuries Whitstable men still mostly called their boats yawls although they had become larger smacks of around 40ft, carvel built with counter sterns and with topmasts to provide more light weather sail area. They were also constructed of massive frames and deadwood to provide the strength necessary for their frequent grounding on the Shore. The older clinker-built smacks were often doubled for longer life and then sometimes had a third phase when, the constant grounding and rising with the tides causing too many leaks, the boats were sold away to places like Faversham and Gillingham where mud berths gave another lease of life.

It was, as Harold Rowden said, an alarming experience to be in a smack when she took the ground on the ebb or floated on the young flood in any kind of swell: 'you thought the boat was breaking up'. Harold was a well known figure in the whelking business for many years and a popular lecturer in local history. He had started by being apprenticed to Edwin Foad on *Mary Ann* (F 115). Another valuable source of information here was 'Skipper' Stroud who took to writing his experiences for *Coast and Country* magazine, which led me to him. He generously gave access to his so far unpublished autobiography which records a full life always connected with the sea. He was one of seven brothers, five of whom went crewing on the 'big yachts' of the 1920s and 1930s. Sidney 'Smoker' Stroud started at the age of 19 on the *Britannia* and by 23 was bosun of the Royal yacht. At one stage, in 1931, three of the Stroud brothers, Skipper, Harold and Sidney, were crewing together in Sir Thomas Lipton's J class *Shamrock V* (Sidney having taken part in the 1930 America's Cup races on the other side of the Atlantic).

Smacksmen from other places usually recognised Whitstable craft not only by certain subtleties of lines and rig but also by two more obvious characteristics: the smack's boat towing well astern on a long painter to a ringbolt in the stem, and by the removable dredging ports in the smacks' bulwarks, the smarter vessels always having them secured in place by lanyards when not in use.

Some of the older smacks needed a man constantly on the pumps when they were sailing and at least one, the Seasalter and Ham's *Czarina* (F 131), had been clinker, doubled and then planked over again before she was finally sold away in 1923. She was delivered to a buyer at Mersea for just £12, the towing job being done by Skipper Stroud in the *Seasalter* entirely under sail; an eventful trip which has been described in an article written by Skipper before he died and eventually published in *Bygone Kent* (March 1987). Before taking over *Seasalter*, Skipper spent a few months after being demobbed in 1919 on the watchboat *Three Brothers* (F 134) and then the *Sydney* (F 110). These old smacks were reckoned to be approaching their century in years afloat, their lines giving a hint of the cod's head and mackerel tail hull form of the 18th century. Later research has borne this out, indicating that the *Sydney* was built at Whitstable in 1828.

The largest of the Whitstable smacks was the 51.8ft* *Seasalter* (F 322) built at Whitstable in the 1870s. She was 47ft on the keel with a beam of 14.2ft, hold depth of 7.8ft and with registered tonnage of 29.07. Before World War I she had made regular trips to Falmouth, where the Company had oyster beds, to fetch brood to relay at Whitstable or Essex. By the time Skipper had her she was used mainly for the Essex run with occasional trips to Holland.

The weekly sails to the Essex grounds, at Burnham, Creeksea or West Mersea, were usually started on Wednesday and they reckoned to finish loading with brood in Essex by the Friday morning, returning to Whitstable by that evening so as to re-lay the young oysters on the grounds on Saturday morning. There was a standing practice that they called at the Swin Middle lightship on the way to deliver newspapers and collect the crew's mail.

In March 1922 Skipper Stroud made a run to Colinsplaat in Holland in 16 hours through snow squalls. Pressing on under reefed mainsail and topsail the short steep seas worried the smack and eventually the bowsprit sprang so they had to reef it by a couple of holes. Returning heavily laden with oysters they were rolling the boom end in the water. On topping up the boom to prevent it breaking, the gaff broke instead. They had to make an emergency repair to the gaff by lashing on two windlass handspikes and sailed home from the North Hinder on that bitter March day still under reefed mainsail and topsail, sighting no other vessel for the whole of the voyage home.

* This may be waterline length rather than overall.

Opposite: Regatta day at Whitstable in Edwardian times. In the centre with yard topsail is the bawley *Blackball* (F 129) and on the extreme left is the smack *Mary & Nellie* (F 45).
(Douglas West Studios)

The carrier smack *Thomas Foord* (F 99). Note the raised bulwarks on her quarters indicating deep sea work. This photograph was taken on the opening day of the oyster season with directors of the company and invited merchants aboard for the tasting ceremony. (Douglas West Studios)

One of the renowned 'Skillingers', *Seasalter*, had been built originally for Henry Gann (who later formed the Seasalter and Ham Oyster Company) and Skipper's father Ernest crewed on her as a young man in the North Sea oyster fishery.

The fishermen's word Skillinger derives from the natural oyster grounds on the Terschelling Bank off the Friesians. Powerful and seaworthy craft as the Skillingers were, three Colne-crewed smacks were lost when a fierce gale blew up and caught them on these dangerous shoals in March 1883. Another two smacks were lost the following year and the Essexmen mostly decided that they would avoid Terschelling thereafter and go down-Channel instead. Although Rochester, Milton and Sheppey men also went away for the North Sea and Channel deep water oyster and scallop dredging very little is recorded of those brave days.

Whitstable had four or five shipyards within recent living memory and as these and the oyster companies were the only major sources of employment in the town they tended to set the somewhat low level of wages. It was remembered that the pay of skilled men was at one time 21/- (£1.05) a week and the apprentices' pay only 3/6 (17½p).

The two biggest yards (known as Upper and Lower Yards) were owned by the Whitstable Shipbuilding Company and were capable of repairing the fleet of collier brigs trading out of Whitstable. These yards, together with the yards of Thomas Collar & Sons and Richard and Charles Perkins, also built most of the local smacks. Both Skipper Stroud and Harold Rowden had vivid memories of the Collars' yard, including the sawpit with the bottom sawyer wearing a sack over his head as some protection against the shower of sawdust.

The Collar brothers were charitable men in a practical way, often handing out bread and jam and cocoa breakfasts to the poorer children on their way to school, as Harold Rowden could testify. (According to the *Kentish Gazette* of 1895 the Collars were doing this as long ago as the great freeze-up of that year when many men were out of work.) Collars' smacks were much admired locally for their sailing performance and handsome lines with fine runs and quarters, although the family's charitable habits made for problems in financing work in hand. When Lammas Emptage was having *Rosa & Ada* (F 105) built he had to find £60 for the planks needed to complete the hull. But then Whitstable smacks must have consumed vast amounts of timber especially in the massive scantlings of the deadwood and frames. Some smacks used at Whitstable, like *Beatrice* and *Clyde* (F 7), were brought down from Essex. The first of these had strengthening frames put in but *Clyde* did not and the regular pounding on the Flats soon took its toll so that she needed constant pumping.

Before leaving the subject of the timber used in the yawls, it is worth noting that two of the few remaining Whitstable craft still afloat, *Rosa & Ada* and *Gamecock* (F 76) are reputed to have had their keels cut from the same baulk of timber. On the death of Henry Collar in 1939 at the age of 91, the *Fishing News* noted that his father, John Collar, had designed many fast smacks including *Rival* and *Slipper*. Another was *Royal Sovereign* (F 140); and at the end the Collar brothers constructed one of the few surviving Whitstable smacks, and the last to be built at Whitstable, *Gamecock* (F 76) for Ernest Stroud, launched on 14th June 1907. The Collars are thought to have supplied one or two of the Ramsgate smacks as well.

Among the multitude of counter-sterned smacks at Whitstable were a few bawleys, boomsail-rigged. These included *Erato* (F 127) owned by Emptage, *Skylark* (F 139), *Thomas & Alfred* (F 1) an old Medway bawley owned by the Luckhurst family, *Blackball* (F 129) owned by the Seasalter & Ham Company, *Clio* (F 284) and *Stella* (F 12). All of these seemed to have been at Whitstable during or before World War I. After that war came *Francois* (F 3), a Gill bawley previously on the Medway, a second *Skylark* (F 117), *Honey Bee* (F 54), owned by George Spratt, *Wings of Morning* (F 39) owned by Dick Gascoigne and *Fiona*.

I shall make no attempt to trace the final history of the Whitstable smacks that were sold away (or sometimes sailed away by local fishermen settling elsewhere) in the 1920s and 1930s, except to say that several found their way to the Medway. A jobbing boatbuilder, 'Blucher' Baker of Lower Gillingham, bought up a number of these craft for conversion to yachts. Some were familiar names in my boyhood, such as *Ibis* (F 52), *Satellite* (F 11) and *Phantom* (F 124). The last ended her days hulked off Gillingham Strand, but the *Satellite*, first registered in 1874 by J. Kemp, small (28ft by 10ft), clinker originally and doubled, was sold again to become a Gravesend shrimper. She had been owned at one time in the 1920s by the brothers Phil and Arthur Peacock who lived in one of the tall 18th century houses in Christmas Street, long demolished; they also

Another carrier smack, and 'Skillinger', *Seasalter* (FM 322) also with raised bulwarks on the quarters. This photograph was taken in 1923 with *Seasalter* arriving in Essex to load oyster brood for relaying on the Ham & Seasalter grounds. (T. Tearle)

owned the ex-Whitstable smacks *John & Mary* (F 16) and *Kate* (F 87), a Collar smack, a few years later. Their father, Philip, had bought the *Phantom*, a smack of 1869 vintage in 1921.

It should be said that Whitstable, particularly in a north or north westerly gale, is an exposed anchorage and it was desirable then for the smacks to use heavy coir cope springs to take the shocks of the mooring chain off the windlass and bitts. The usual method was to attach an iron dog (two-clawed hook) on a few links of chain to a coir spring and hook the dog into the mooring chain just inside the stem head. The spring was hauled tight enough with a double purchase tackle to get some slack in the mooring chain, the dog was securely lashed in, and the spring made fast round the mast at deck level.

It was hard on the men in the watchboats in such conditions. Arthur Foreman (nicknamed Dido, as was his father) told me that he would never go on the Seasalter & Ham's watchboats. The few extra pence earned was not enough compensation for the hours spent heaving up and down on moorings offshore. Skipper Stroud, who was prepared to earn the one shilling a night on a watchboat, also declined to pitch and roll at the moorings in a blow. He would slip the buoy and run for shelter 'under the Ness' at Sheppey, knowing that no oyster poachers would be at sea in that weather anyway.

To describe the life of a Whitstable oysterman I cannot do better than draw upon Skipper Stroud's autobiography: 'As a youngster I went as fourth hand on *Gamecock* and worked "on the bow". This meant that whatever I caught dredging was kept separate and the boat took one quarter share of what it was sold for. The share system in the Whitstable oyster smacks worked this way. The crew normally consisted of three men and the proceeds of the catches divided into four shares, one each for the men and one for the boat and gear. Therefore, if you had a fourth hand working on the bow he paid over a quarter of his proceeds. For the best part of one year I worked only one dredge, the others working two dredges each. These dredges weighed 28lb before being rigged. The rigging consisted of the "ground" which was made of galvanised wire rings, shut together like chain-mail. The rings were about 1¼ or 1½ inches in diameter and each man made his own ground; there were many sore and blistered hands when these were made. At each side were "side-sticks", and a "catch-stick" was fastened along the bottom which helped you to empty the contents of the dredge on deck for culling. The "upper" was a net made of hemp twine, the mesh being about an inch or so square and was laced to the ground with leather or hide thongs.

'Working on the bow was much harder than working abaft the rigging, for the bow was much higher above the waterline. By the time the heel of the dredge was on the rail the rest of the dredge and its contents were out of the water and consequently heavier to lift. Later at the age of 14 I was working three dredges, catching mussels by the ton for the farmers to spread on their land for fertiliser. Four men could dredge up and load below decks about 10 tons of mussels in one working

Another Whitstable Regatta day photograph. *Emmeline* (F 14) leads the group of smacks. *Monarch* (F 80) is in the centre of the picture and *Victory* (F 64) is on the left (note her topmast well bowsed down). (Douglas West Studios)

tide – which would be under six hours – then sail back to harbour and unload. After cleaning up the boat we would get out of the harbour again, if there was enough water, and onto moorings ready to start again next morning. The price paid by farmers for mussels pre-1914 was 10/- (50p) a ton.'

As Sidney Stroud pointed out, in the days of the Whitstable free dredgers when it was a matter of dredging a daily stint of oysters, the men might have to spend only two or three hours out on the grounds. But the Stroud brothers were brought up on six hours continuous dredging on the Ham & Seasalter Company's grounds. Sidney started at the age of 15 and recalled vividly in his retirement how hard it was on the hands at first hauling on the bass dredge warps embedded with sand and small pieces of shell from the seabed. Among the remedies for sore and split hands were petroleum jelly and 'Dutch Drops' oil.

In sailing days the smacks usually worked six dredges in pairs as already described, the bowman having the two largest, two slightly smaller ones for the 'midships man and the skipper handling still lighter ones aft. Mostly the dredging would not start until two hours after high water and became easier towards low water as the length of warp could be shortened and the stopper moved down accordingly. Warps were attached to the iron ring through the heel of the dredge by a fisherman's bend; they were of four-strand bass rope some 14 fathoms long, although not normally allowed to run out to their full extent. Besides the fact that the depth of water on the grounds was sometimes as little as 1½ fathoms and rarely more than four or five, by staggering the lengths of warp run out the problem of dredges getting foul of each other was less likely to happen. Traditionally the bowman worked the shortest pair of warps, the 'midships man's were a little longer and the skipper's on the stern quarter were the longest. It was to compensate for the different weight of the warp lengths in hauling in that the longest warps were bent to the lighter dredges; also the light dredges needed longer warps to 'bite'.

After the dredges were shot and allowed to run out to the desired distance the warps were hitched to the smack's rail by breakable stoppers. These were made by unlaying something like 5ft lengths of bass rope and then laying-up a couple of yarns again. The stoppers were taken through a hole in the scuppers, round a stanchion and fastened with a rolling hitch. If a dredge got 'fast' to an obstruction on the seabed the stopper would break and the rest of the dredge warp, buoyed at the end with a piece of wood, could be allowed to run out for later recovery. This way no gear was damaged unnecessarily. The dredge buoy was roughly tapered at one end and drilled so that the end of the warp could be taken through and stoppered with a figure-of-eight knot, the tapering being intended to make the buoy float more upright on the surface of the sea.

The dredging drill was to empty one dredge on deck, shoot it again and then cull out, all the gash being 'shaded' out through the ports in the bulwarks, then haul up the next dredge and so on. The oysters retained after culling out were chipped away from pieces of culch dredged up with the heavy oysterman's knife, his cultick.

When dredging under power came in there were still three men in a boat's crew but they had to work three dredges each and, as Arthur Foreman told me, it was more exhausting work too because, instead of having a fairly long break while the smack sailed back to the next strip of grounds to be dredged, the motor boat covered the return trip more quickly so shortening the break. The powered boats usually dredged heading down-tide working two dredges from the stern and two from each quarter. Derrick West, who worked for the Seasalter & Ham Company until the end in 1972, recalled that at low water slack they could actually circle round dredging under power.

The culled oysters were first measured into bushels by being put into baskets called 'dockers' and then into net bags. At the end of the day the oysters were taken ashore to the company's sheds in the smacks' boats, the men rowing 'London-fashion' (more precisely, randan style), the man, or men, on the middle thwart pulling a pair of oars and two men with an oar each on the other two thwarts pulling on opposite sides. The forward oarsman was responsible for guiding the boat, adjusting the steering by pulling harder or easing off as required.

All the oystermen had similar recollections of what happened as the end of the working day approached. Skipper Stroud: 'As we were the flagship (aboard *Seasalter*) with the foreman of the grounds aboard – he

was an uncle, Harry Stroud, nicknamed "Blugs" – all the other boats looked to us and watched our movements as it drew to knock-off time. As time started when the first boat arrived on the grounds, all sail was set to get out there and once there more appropriate working sail was set. Towards the end of the day the sail would be changed again for getting back into the Bay. As soon as they saw us getting a bigger jib or topsail they would follow suit and as soon as they saw the "flag go up", which was a sack slipped over the end of a boat-hook, they were "in sheets and off".'

Skipper had a good story about his uncle, Alfred 'Jumbo' Stroud. 'It was on the Pollard and not a breath of wind. All the smacks were kedge-anchored and the boats were "all tow". This meant that three of the four crew went in the boat with a dredge which they towed by rowing since the smack could not herself be used for "drudging". My uncle was skipper of the *Czarina* and she was at anchor with the rest of the fleet. She had not set her jackyard topsail but only her small one. Mr Gann, the managing director of the company, came up in a motor-boat doing his rounds of the fleet. Seeing *Czarina* with only a small topsail set, idled by and said "Why haven't you got your big topsail set Jumbo?", who replied, "Because there ain't enough bloody wind for what's up there now".'

By 1924 the 'great oyster mortality' (later attributed to a small parasite, hexamita) was severe and the companies cut the men's pay by half to 7/6 (37½p) a day (the dredgermen's previous 15/- (75p) a day was half War Bonus and they now had to revert to basic pay). 'There was nothing we could do about it. There was no industry in the town and earnings by the other smacks not employed by the two companies were even less profitable. No five-fingers or mussels were required by the farmers and no more Roman Cement was being manufactured and so no dredging for stone.' After a few months of earning only 7/6 (37½p) a day plus an extra shilling (5p) skipper's allowance, he decided that to support his family properly a change had to be made and signed up with the Orient Line as able seaman.

Any attempt to describe life at Whitstable in the latter days of working sail would be incomplete without mention of the eagerly awaited occasions when the smacksmen raced in the annual regattas. There were two, the Town Regatta held off Tankerton and the West End Regatta at the other end of the beach organised by local businessmen. The smacks raced in three classes, the two classes of local 'yawls' starting in the usual way but the Essex smacks being started with their crews on the beach. On being given the starting gun the men tumbled into their small boats and rowed with fast powerful strokes to their anchored smacks. Arthur Foreman recalled that occasionally the sails of the waiting smacks could

Opposite: Ernest Stroud and his sons aboard *Gamecock* in 1928. The smack is at Anderson, Rigden & Perkins' yard having a Kelvin sleeve-valve engine installed. Left to right are his seven sons, Alfred, Albert ('Skipper'), Harold, Sidney, Ernest, Jack and Fred. (A. Stroud)

Two recent photographs of the Whitstable Oyster Company's building of 1896 which stands on the sea wall with the Pearson's Arms pub and oyster bar close by.

be seen to magically start to rise before the crew had clambered aboard to split into teams for dealing with anchor and halyards. It was suspected that there was sometimes a small boy already on board who was impatient to be off. Arthur remembered *Gamecock*, *Rosa & Ada* and *Emmeline* (F 14) as successful racing smacks in the later years. All were built by Collar and still afloat today. *Emmeline*, 38.5ft by 12.2ft, was built for Harry Whorlow in 1904 but was owned latterly by Vic Foreman. However the ex-Colchester smack *Amorel* (F 10) was generally reckoned to be the crack boat. The Stroud's *Gamecock* came into her own in very light winds, ghosting to the front of the fleet. She won in the first class of the last regatta before the 1914-18 war; the winnings, six guineas and a silver teapot. In fact the men had a standing agreement to share out the prize money whoever won so that they all got some pay for the day. The champion smack was then called 'cock of the walk' and given a copper cockerel to use as a mast bob. But, as *Gamecock* already had a plywood silhouette of a gamecock as a vane with a red tail of cloth about a foot long, the Strouds did not bother to change their masthead cock for their championship year.

Of course there were many other events besides yawl racing on regatta days, including yacht races and randan rowing races, the greasy pole competition and swimming races for all age groups. The day often ended with a bang – the blowing up of an old ship's boat by the local salvage company.

In the later regattas of the 1930s Norman Cuckow raced with Johnny Warner's crew on *Monarch* (F 80) against a field of eight or nine smacks. The skipper was fussy when racing, insisting on hatches being closed and staying at the helm all the time calling out his orders. Norman and a member of *Monarch*'s usual crew worked the mainsheet together. The course was triangular, from the harbour out to and round a watchboat and some other mark, a distance of about nine miles which they went round twice if there was enough wind. *Monarch* was frequently placed in the results, which was more than full compensation for the hands made sore by heaving on the coarse ropes on the working boats of that era.

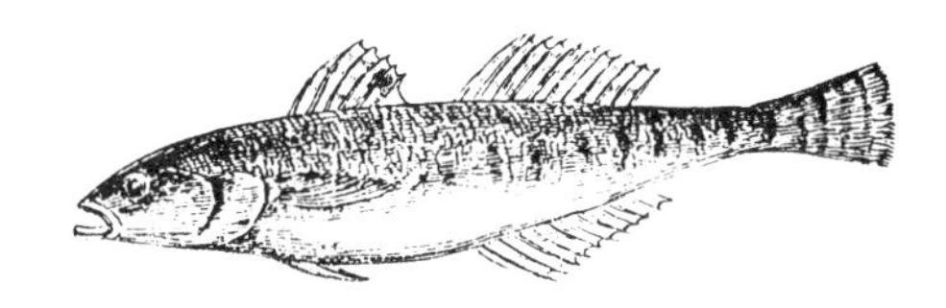

The Whitstable smack *Pet* (F 67) becalmed with jib sheets dragging idly in the water. There is evidently no urgent need to move judging by the attitudes of the crew and the fact that the topmast is lowered. (National Maritime Museum)

# 8

# *The Flatsmen*

As we have seen in the previous chapter, as early as the 1790s membership of the Whitstable Oyster Company had to be restricted and, according to A.O. Collard writing at the turn of this century, there remained a large body of men who obtained what he called a 'comfortable living' working as flatsmen. They dredged for oysters on the common grounds of the Kentish Flats (in competition with members of the Company who frequently dredged on the Flats themselves to supplement their earnings) and could turn to whelking, cockling, and dredging mussels and five-fingers to sell to the local farmers for manure according to need and opportunity.

In the last few years before World War I there were still about seventy smacks and bawleys at Whitstable and at the close of the spring oyster season perhaps eight or ten would spend the summer mainly trawling, and some of the remaining boats would carry on dredging the Flats. Although out of season, those dredging could still sell both fully grown oysters and brood for relaying on the two companies' grounds (the Whitstable Oyster Company and the Seasalter & Ham Oyster Company working in association). Whelks were of course sold for eating, as were mussels if they were large enough and the flatsmen received 2/- (10p) a bushel for these. Two smacks were used frequently for whelk trapping (called trotting) and one or two for 'stoning' – dredging up Roman stone for cement making.

Many of the 'oystermen' had to find work ashore out of the dredging season, mostly on local farms, in casual fruit-picking and hopping. Others gave holiday visitors rowing trips from the beach in smacks' boats kept smart for this work. But those with their own smacks could go trawling and Skipper Stroud put his recollections of this in a letter, from which I quote. 'We in *Gamecock*, together with old Sammy Emptage in *Rosa & Ada* as well as old "Shalico" Rigden in *Erato*, would put our fish trawls aboard for six weeks' trawling. After that it was ashore with the fish trawl and aboard with the shrimp gear. We would be joined by half a dozen others with their shrimp gear aboard. There would be Johnny Warner in *St Agnes*, Bentley Rigden in *Stella*, Bill Stroud in *Eva*, "Crutchy" Gambell in *Skylark*, "Whacker" Friend in *Shamrock* and "Tears & Smiles" Shingleston in *Bluebell*. And I must mention "Dubby" Rigden in *Freda* as she was the only boat at that time to have an auxiliary engine but was only allowed to use it to get to and fro the fishing grounds. There were several occasions when we in the *Gamecock* have been grateful for a tow home.

'It was always a chancy start for shrimps, trying first on the Kentish Flats, down the Gore Channel or along the Woolpack, heaving overboard the tell-tale to see if there were enough shrimps to warrant shooting the trawl. If not it would be an early start on the tide the next day to get out to the Gilman by high water, shoot the shrimp trawl at the Gilman buoy and tow down outside the Girdler. If it was a spring tide and wind from a westerly quarter we used to drop away head to wind with both parts of the warp in the fore hawse to tow slow enough, then haul our gear at the Girdler Elbow buoy, go down through Alexandra Channel, shoot our gear again at the North Tongue buoy and finish the tide down Princes Channel; then it would be punch back all the way home.' It was very important to know where to trawl. And as Arthur Foreman pointed out, any later in the season than May, seaweed, especially the long golden tapes of pipeweed, could ruin the fishing by clogging the net. Also a heavy haul of five-fingers could mean having to cut the trawl open to get rid of them. Experienced smacksmen often tried an oyster dredge as a tell-tale before deciding when and where it was safe to shoot the trawl.

The other curse of sailing fishermen was of course a dying wind. 'When working down the Princes Channel or the Queens Channel oft times the wind died away to a calm. Then we got into the boat, two of us, leaving Father aboard, rowed the twelve miles or so back to Whitstable, got the shrimps packed and away, then back into the boat again and row back to the smack. Sometimes a light breeze would have brought her nearer home and we would not have to row so far, but if it were still calm it meant that once we got back it was to row the smack home, Father rowing aboard the smack with a long sweep.' On these occasions the man in the smack's boat usually lashed its stem under the taffrail of their smack and pushed her along, a more effective method than towing. Sidney Stroud confirmed his brother's account of this technique. He once rowed thus in the smack's boat for six hours, all the way from Birchington to Whitstable, his father at the smack's helm with a sweep lashed to the rail and the third hand pushing a sweep against the shrouds for'ard.

Skipper's and Sidney's father Ernest Stroud at one time kept a pub, The Royal Native in Harbour Street. He was also a shellfish and smoked fish dealer; the big copper in the scullery was used for boiling the cockles, mussels, winkles and whelks, while the coalhouse was also a smoke-hang for curing herrings and sprats. A good supply of oak chips was readily obtained from the four shipyards in the town and the bloaters and sprats were cured properly to a dark brown colour.

Another activity Skipper mentions in his autobiography is making mushroom ketchup. 'We used to get countrymen coming in with baskets of mushrooms which my father bought cheaply, but of course the old chaps could get a good tuck-in cheaply as well. At that time you could have a pint of beer, a big hunk of bread and cheese and an onion, a

The Seasalter & Ham's ketch *Speedwell* in the 1920s. The man on the left is throwing his dredge. Behind him is Charles Camburn the engineer. The next man along is about to pull his full dredge over the rail and the man on the extreme right, Sibert Shingleston, is resting the dredge on the rail by its heel. (D. West)

packet of five Woodbines and a box of matches, and have a penny change out of sixpence.' Skipper also wrote of selling bloaters and smoked sprats from a basket around the town as a boy. The smoked sprats, a typical November or December meal of the time, cost 3d for a bundle of twenty. After the family had to leave the pub in 1907 (when the number of licensed premises was reduced by official decree) they had to live more cheaply, relying more on 'rock beef', the local name for shellfish – mussels, clams, whelks and cockles – which they gathered themselves. But they also had their new smack *Gamecock* to help earn a living and Ernest Stroud went fishing in her until he was 77 years of age.

Skipper wrote: 'During the summer when shrimps were plentiful I used to go round during the lunch hour from school with a basket and a stamped half-pint glass measure selling our fresh shrimps at 2d a pint. They had to be that day's shrimps too. You could not fool the local people with shrimps caught the previous day as they could tell by the feel of them. This meant working mostly at nights and getting ashore between eight and ten in the morning to get the shrimps packed and away by trains to Canterbury, Herne Bay, Margate, Ramsgate, Deal, Dover and Folkestone, and sometimes to Ashford and Chatham. Any surplus catch could be sent to Billingsgate but the returns were usually poor. However, out of season, if there were any shrimps to be caught, prices in Billingsgate would soar beyond any price that could be obtained locally. It was the same with fish. When fish trawling was in full

A Sheringham crab boat with dipping lugsail set. Evidently one of the boats brought down from Norfolk in the 1890s to go whelking from Whitstable. (Douglas West Studios)

swing we used to sell the smaller flatfish all gutted and cleaned and strung up for 3d a score, or a skate weighing up to 10lb for 9d. People would say "I'll buy one if you'll skin it". Whereas, by just sending the wings to Billingsgate packed with bits of broken ice on top skate wings would fetch eight to ten shillings (50p) and sometimes more for a stone weight.'

This would be in about 1910. While on the subject of prices, Skipper had this to say on pre-World War I oyster prices: 'During the winter months when *Gamecock*'s crew consisted of my father and us two boys we were marketing our own oysters. The four sizes being 5/- (25p) per hundred for the best, 3/6 (17½p) per hundred for the second size, 2/6 (12½p) for the third and 1/6 (7½p) for "buttons". On Sunday morning I would be detailed to go down to the store (on the beach) and bring home what oysters were left, irrespective of size. Father would open as many as three hundred while the bacon was frying. The oysters would be fried in the bacon fat until the edges started to crisp, that was enough. What a breakfast for a family!'

After a spell in the Merchant Navy, Skipper returned to Whitstable in March 1925 and as the fish trawling season was just starting decided to try his hand skippering his cousin Albert Ashby's smack, *Swift* (F 40). In his own words: 'It was early April when we eventually started trawling and we did very well financially, managing a good average weekly wage, but as the weeks went by and the fish shifted out into deeper water this meant many more hours out as you needed to be away almost two hours before high water to get to the fishing grounds to get your trawl shot as soon as the tide turned for the ebb, getting the best of the tide. We used to shoot on the first of the ebb, tow our trawl down along the Cant, hauling before we got to the Redsand, then sailing across the Knob Channel shooting the trawl again and towing for the rest of the tide down along the Barrow sands just inside the deep water line as far as the Mid-Barrow Light. By then the ebb would have finished. Then it was a good few hours knocking back home. We then tried out another fishing ground, down the Queens Channel and down along the Woolpack, finishing the ebb down along the north side of Margate Sands. If the wind was favourable then shoot again and tow on the first of the flood up along the south side of Margate Sands and the Hook Sands. Towards the end we were doing this two-handed; one of the original crew had found the hours too much.'

If the weather looked threatening and the men could not decide whether to go out fishing they would often leave their beach huts and stroll along to The Pearson's Arms to confer in comfort and 'consult the glass'. When the tides were around mid-day they were inclined to be less venturesome as this could mean a long wait hove-to offshore until there was enough water to return to moorings. They would often rather choose to get away in the early hours of the following morning, saving the last of the tide off the Flats.

Whitstable Bay is favoured by having something of a natural breakwater in the form of The Street, the long bank of stones and shingle stretching out almost due north from the beach. If the wind was easterly

Tom Taylor aboard his whelk boat in the 1920s. He is emptying a pot into a wooden cask before putting the whelks into a wash-sized net bag. (D. West)

Two more ex-Sheringham boats unloading on the beach. The oar ports in the top strake used for carrying the boats up and down the beach can be seen clearly. The boat on the right is *Lily* (FM 60). She was 17.9ft long, built at Sheringham in 1906 for Robert Cox.
(Douglas West Studios)

it gave some protection just as the moored smacks had to take the ground on the ebb or lift again with the rising tide. However it gave little protection against a northerly or north westerly gale. The Seasalter & Ham Company's smacks' mooring chains were 35 fathoms long, the lower 15 fathoms of ¾in bar chain (shackled to the ground chain from the buried anchor or screw), the upper 15 fathoms slightly smaller, and with a five fathom length of lighter chain to lead through the hawse and round the windlass. Yet despite such heavy ground gear many a smack broke loose in northerly gales and drove ashore, including Jimmy Stroud's *Rebel* (F 93). She came ashore close to her owner's beach hut where the heavy seas first pounded in her decks and then broke her up. Tradition has it that on one black day no less than 14 smacks drove ashore.

To end this section I will quote from Skipper Stroud's memories of five-fingering and stoning on the Flats: 'Starfish are much lighter than mussels and contained much more fluid. Consequently a lot of weight was lost overnight after the five-fingers were caught, the fluid draining down into the bilges so that you were constantly pumping out ship. Also the hold had to be fitted up into "pounds" for the stability of the vessel. There were two long boards which ran fore and aft the length of the hold and these were divided athwartships both in the centre of the hold and both sides under the decks.

'We worked four dredges each. These were lighter than the normal oyster dredges and the bits were designed not to scrape the sea-bottom but only pick up stuff on top. The net meshes and ground rings were larger too. It took several days to get a full load and often you would not manage more than five tons in three or four days because of the wastage in fluid weight. The Essexmen were known to manage it in three or even two days by working all daylight hours. Sometimes the Whitstable men would land a half load before it dried out too much. If you had five-fingers on board for three days or more the stench below was terrible and it would turn the paintwork a leaden colour. The World War I price paid for starfish was 18/- (90p) a ton and £2 a ton after the war.

'At the end of a season of five-fingering you would take advantage of the first calm day and have the floors up in the hold, take all the iron ballast up on deck and thoroughly clean everywhere. Then re-stow the ballast and lay the floors again. Otherwise you would never have a sweet smelling boat again. Although some people just chucked buckets of water below and pumped out.

'Another thing we did, although I only remember one other boat doing the same, was "stoning". This was dredging for the stones used to make Roman cement; it was heavy work and only done as a last resort. This stone was the petrified material left when the sea had washed away the London clay cliffs. The stone from Warden Point on Sheppey was harder than that off Swalecliffe just below Whitstable. We were paid 8/- (40p) a ton for Sheppey stone and 6/6 (32½p) for Swalecliffe stone. Working out from "back of the Island" was harder work because the Sheppey stone did not break so easily and it was difficult to get some of the larger ones aboard. Sometimes you would have to get someone to help get a piece up to two hundredweight on deck when a lump got wedged between the dredge bit and the "warbling" (the cross piece of dredge frame, in effect the top of dredge mouth to which the net is secured). Having got anything between eight and ten tons in the one tide we would sail up to Faversham where it was unloaded to be fired in the kilns, the powder later being mixed with mud and used for cement manufacture.

'It is a long winding creek up to Faversham wharf and if it was a head wind it meant being put ashore with a bow line and towing the smack up the creek. Once at the wharf the stone was unloaded while the tide was high and if possible get away down to Whitstable again. More often than not though we slept on the cabin lockers. The top two were about 2ft wide but the lower ones only about 15 inches wide so not the height of comfort.'

### *'Whilking'*

In the 1890s Whitstable saw an example of the periodical migrations of fishing families from one part of the British coastline to another. In this case it was the arrival of some of the Sheringham men to take over the whelk fishing with their superior skill and equipment. Whelking (always pronounced 'whilking' by the fishing families and many of their customers) was mostly done by trotting before the Norfolk men arrived. Trotting meant one day catching shore crabs for bait and the next, weather permittting, putting down long lines with pieces of broken crab threaded through twine, to which the 'whilks' obstinately attached themselves and could thus be pulled to the surface.

Bob Foad and Derrick West shooting the whelk pots from *Floreat* (F 91). This photograph illustrated a newspaper article in 1979. (Whitstable Times)

The Sheringham men's method, which they claimed to have devised themselves (possibly from seeing whelks get trapped in their crab pots), was to use a small pot put down in 'shanks' of about 25 at a time, lifted and re-baited every day. The whelk pots used now are still much the same, a beehive shape formed by eight curved iron rods ('bows') set in a 13in diameter perforated iron base and welded at the top to an 8in diameter ring, the whole pot standing about 1ft high. Replacements at first had to be ordered from Norfolk although the local forges could repair the bows when necessary, and later on learnt to make the whole frame.

The sides of the pot are formed by weaving rope through the bows, building up about twenty turns. In the days of natural fibre ropes a generation ago the whelkers sent away to Lowestoft for cheap used rope from old herring nets, called 'three part back',* but this stuff only lasted about a year even though the pots were dipped in tar and allowed to weather after the rope was woven through. The whelk bait is held inside the pot on the 'bar', a loop of cord. To rig this, both ends of the cord are passed either side of a bow on one side of the pot and an overhand (or thumb) knot made in the cord, the ends of which are passed through a 'button', then out through the other side of the pot and tied tightly. The button was originally a kind of grommet with a sisal cord half-hitched all round with string about two inches in diameter, but

* Backrope was the foot rope of herring drift nets.

The whelker *Floreat* photographed recently. These Whitstable-built boats still show their origins in the Sheringham crab boats.

Sketch of Whitstable whelk pots and marker buoy by Leslie Hill. One of the heavy perforated iron bases is leaning against the pot on the left.

nowadays the bait is firmly held against the knot on the bar by a pierced square of rubber tyre or piece of hose. The whelks find their way up the side of the pot and down through the hole at the top from which hangs a short tube of net known as the 'crinny' (from crinoline).

In sailing days a two-man crew worked the small double-ended whelkers which some called cobles and were in fact the Sheringham crabbers sailed down from Norfolk by their owners. A full load of pots normally amounted to 125, five shanks of 25 pots, although some men preferred four shanks of 30 each. They worked in up to six fathoms of water, mainly on clay bottoms (never rocks), and shot across the tide with about 50ft of rope (the 'tow') between each pot, each having its own loop of rope called the 'strop', a buoy at either end of the shank. They were lifted every day and baited with broken red-shelled crab or fish pieces: skate or red (smoked) herring were the best. Today the remaining two whelk boats use only skate backs and salt down a stock whenever they are caught by the local trawlermen. At the present time the smaller whelks are found inshore at Swalecliffe and in the Stone Channel off the Reculver. The bigger ones, some 'as big as a cup practically' are farther out at the West Spaniard and towards Queens Channel.

The pots are generally left down all the year now, except for a shank at a time which is brought ashore for repair and cleaning up, including the removal of barnacles (called 'chitters' at Whitstable). As in the past, spring is perhaps the best time of year for whelking but in the right temperature range whelks can be caught at any time of year. They will not 'crawl' when the water is too cold or warm, although it is now possible to find them with powered boats in deeper water towards the Redsand when the weather is warm.

The whole business of 'whilking' was made much easier with powered craft as hauling and shooting the pots is best done by slowly stemming the tide with the engine throttled down to just the right speed. The fishermen who had to rely on sail and oar had to be careful not to go too fast in case the pots tipped over and the whelks crawled free.

Bill West, in his nineties, remembered the start of it, coming down from Sheringham with his mother in the train in 1896 when he was five years old. The men sailed their crab boats down, four families at first and three or four others later (some had tried Dungeness first). Apart from the Wests there were the Cox, Bishop, Johnson and Green families among others; and a difficult time they had of it at first. The whelkers were regarded as a nuisance by the oyster dredgers as the long shanks of pots stretching across the Flats often got foul of the dredges. Moreover, Whitstable, like most other small towns at that time, looked upon strangers with suspicion which sometimes moved into hostility. Bill West spoke of people jeering and laughing at the Sheringham families in the High Street where the broad Norfolk accents would have set them apart at once. It must have been hard for a small boy starting school in those early years. Eventually though the incomers were accepted into the community (some changing their accents to become less conspicuous) with no actual violence between the men but some shouting from boat to boat and the occasional rope shank cut through by irate smacksmen.

The Whitstable smack *Rosa & Ada*'s barrel capstan and foredeck with bowsprit run in, photographed when she was lying at Hollowshore in 1973.

Dick Norris' *Stormy Petrel* (F 71) in a smart breeze with mainsail triced up. Dick, standing amidships, has owned the smack for 25 years. Built by Richard and Charles Perkins in 1890 she is probably unique among surviving smacks in never having had her deadwood bored for an engine. (R.E. Norris)

The whelk harvest, although good when the Sheringham men first moved to Whitstable, gradually declined and some of the men eventually gave up and worked mainly in the oyster smacks. At the peak there were about a dozen or more 'whilkers' at Whitstable, a mixture of Sheringham crab boats of about 18ft and locally-built boats. These were larger and heavier than the Norfolk craft, the clinker strakes fastened with copper rooves instead of nails; and by the time the local boats were being constructed motors were coming in, single-cylinder Gardners at first.

Bill West's father had his first replacement boat built at Sheringham in 1908 and in the traditional way. She was named *Boy Bill*, after his son, and delivered to Whitstable Harbour by rail. Bill later took her over and worked her by sail and oar. He once won a race in the local regatta in this boat against a field of 'whilkers', giving his winnings to the Canterbury Hospital. The *Boy Bill* (F 104) was 17.8ft long overall with a beam of 6.8ft.

Bill remembered that Henry Johnson also had a new boat built at Sheringham for £90 and delivered by railway. Other Sheringham craft included *John Mathew* (F 33) of 1899 (18ft by 6.9ft) owned by John Green in 1910; *Lloyd George* (F 38) of 1910 (18.9ft by 6.9ft) sold away to Brightlingsea in 1919; and *Theodore* (F 34) (17.9ft by 6.4ft) owned by Harry Whorlow in 1905: all these details from the Faversham Fishing Boat Register.

Harold Rowden started out with an old Norfolk boat, the *Dolphin*, which had originally been sailed down by the Bishop family. After World War II the whelkers were making good money and Harold had a Whitstable boat built, calling her *Audrey Russell* after the BBC broadcaster. All of the last crop of motorised whelk boats built around the 1948/50 period came from Anderson, Rigden & Perkins. They were 22 to 24ft in length with a beam of 8.6ft or so. Sidney Stroud recalled that his *Random Harvest* (F 75) was built by the shipwrights Ernie Wood and Bill 'Cod' Kelsey. Other boats were *Three Brothers* for the three Court brothers, *Ocean Gift* (F 36) for Bob Cox and Hilary Abel, and *Floreat* (F 91); the last two are still being worked by Derrick West, Christopher Bishop and Bob Foad.

The traditional dipping lugsail rig was retained until the end of the sailing era, as was the method of ballasting with sacks of shingle from the beach. In a heavy breeze the two-man crew had to be smart in dipping the lugsail and shifting the halyard fall and the ballast bags to windward on each tack, although in fine settled weather only two sacks of ballast might be shipped.

They worked a wide area of the Estuary; 'along the land' off Sheppey as far as Sheerness to the west and down past the Reculver and Gore Channel towards Margate to the east. Generally the whelks on the Flats are more tender, with whiter flesh, than those found on stonier ground. Bill West's favourite place was in the narrow gut of Stone Channel off Reculver. Other guts where the pots were put down were in 'Church in the Hole' off Warden Point (where the heavier red whelk could be found) and 'House in the Hole' farther along the Sheppey shore. These places yielded bigger whelks than those on the nearby Spile.

The Whitstable smack *Gamecock* being raced by her owner, Bill Coleman, in the 1981 Swale Match. *Gamecock* was built by Collar Brothers and launched on 14 June 1907, the last at Whitstable.
(Chris Davey, Whitstable Times)

At first the Norfolk men carried their boats up the beach as they had for generations on the East Anglian coast. It took six men using three oars pushed through the paired ports in the sheerstrakes. These ports are called 'urrocks' in Norfolk today, an example of the way words can be corrupted within a generation or two. Bill West's version, and probably the current usage of the 1890s, was 'ullocks', and this plainly suggests 'oarlocks', an appropriate name for holes cut into the side of the boat to hold the oar in place when rowing.* Later on the Sheringham men started to keep their boats in Whitstable Harbour and the practice of carrying them up the beach gradually ceased; it would have been impractical anyway for the Whitstable built 'whilkers', constructed with heavier scantlings in the local manner.

The lugsails used on the Sheringham crab boats and retained at Whitstable were cut fairly low but nearly as long as the boat. A good lifting sail, according to Bill West; powerful, too, with good windward abilities when set properly so that rowing was rarely necessary unless the wind dropped.

A good day's catch would be about 25 wash (about 5¼ gallons to the wash). The pots were hauled, culled of crabs and under-sized whelks, and the catch tipped into a wooden bucket. The pots were re-baited and stacked in piles for'ard with the tows neatly flaked down towards the stern, and then shot again across tide in a slightly different position on the seabed. The catch was tipped from the bucket into net bags holding a wash each which on return were carried up the beach in pairs slung from a wooden shoulder yoke. The whelks were, and still are, cooked in the net bags, three at a time in large coppers in huts by the harbour. The boiling fresh water cools a little as the net bags are lowered in and is then brought back to the boil again. After cooking the whelks are spread out on boards to dry and any empty shells are culled out; these are often inhabited by hermit crabs, known locally as 'farmers'. For a long time in sailing days the average price was around 1/6 (7½p) a wash at Billingsgate and most of the catch went there, a few sacks also being sent to the local seaside resorts.

The men augmented their earnings with a little fishing at times, occasionally trying the dabnets fitted with a folding iron ring which closes like a purse when yanked to the surface by its warp. Bill West said the trick was to reach down in the water as far as possible to shorten the rope, then jerk very quickly. A couple of oyster dredges were also kept on board the whelk boats and used when normal business was unproductive. Oysters of any size dredged on the Flats were sold to the Whitstable companies for stocking their grounds.

When the weather was too bad to go out there were usually whelk pots to be roped and tarred and wash nets to be braided from twine ('pot stuff') using figure of eight knots, decreasing towards the bottom. Bill West, like other fishermen of his generation, could recall families linseed oiling their own waterproof clothing. The oiled smocks, or frocks to give

* The word oarlock is apparently still in frequent use today in the United States although rarely over here.

them their older name, were either full length or three-quarter length, in which case they were called short frocks. After oiling, these garments were to be seen swinging in the breeze from clothes lines, a stick through the arms to help them dry out. Some of the men still called their short, waist length fisherman's smocks 'slops' as they do in Norfolk today. For a long time they stuck to their old style sou'westers as well, the ones with the long stiff brim extending down over the back of the neck like American firemen wear. The older boats were rarely painted, mostly tarred all the way up. Some might have the top two or three strakes painted grey but no one bothered to cut in the waterline until very recent times when green or blue top strakes began to be seen.

### *Herne Bay*

Hampton to the west of Herne Bay was the home for generations of a family called Mount who were mainly employed in fishing. Frank Mount set down an interesting account in 1942: *My Recollections of Hampton* which described early 19th century Hampton as just a cottage or two on a headland with one or two boats, including a 'bawly' in which Frank Mount's grandfather fished and, for a while, engaged in smuggling.

In 1864 this all changed when the Herne Bay, Hampton and Reculver Oyster Fishery Company was formed and bought up seven miles of the Flats from Swalecliffe to beyond Reculver, acquired five smacks, laid down stock from France, Holland and Portugal, built a pier 350 yards long and constructed breeding pits, storehouse and 12 cottages for employees. A spur was built from the mainline railway on which trucks were to be run to take the oysters to and fro, with sails for use if the wind was fair. The company also bought out a fish weir, owned by a Mr Downs, and changed the old 'Beehive Inn' into the smarter 'Hampton Oyster Inn'.

The enterprise lasted for 10 years or so until the severe winters of the late 1870s wiped out the oyster stock and the company went into liquidation. After that, and because it is said of erosion caused by the pier, about 30 acres of foreshore headland was lost to the sea, but around 1900 Hampton began to be developed for fashionable homes and as a holiday place. Most longshoremen continued to make a living by various means including bait-digging, lobstering and hiring out boats.

The Mounts however continued fishing and Frank Mount describes memorable occasions when they caught 2,500 sea bass by beating, using a 14ft boat and a seine type net 200 yards long by 20ft in depth. They sold these fish from the beach, making £45, enough to buy a new boat and gear. Another good shoal of sea bass was similarly trapped near the shingle spit of Whitstable Street, by laying the net in a horseshoe shape and beating the fish into the bight. But the Mounts' speciality seems to have been mullet which fed along the Flats in shoals of about a thousand fish. The marks made in the sand as they rooted up weed showed when the fish were present and on the next tide the men went out with their long net to encircle the shoal, reckoning to catch 700 or 800 at a time. The average sized fish was 3lb in weight and they sold for 6d (2½p) per pound at Billingsgate whence they sent the fish by lorry, all packed in ice.

# 9

# *Margate Memories*

*by Don Paterson*

## *The Bawleys*

Cockles, whelks, jellied eel's and shrimps: these were the delicacies loved by Londoners when on holiday at Margate during the first quarter of this century. In consequence the little 7½ acre harbour was jammed with fishing craft and the seafront was an almost continuous line of barrows and stalls.

The bawley fleet was never a very large one but in its heyday there were Ben Redshaw's *Mary* (R 86), Henry Matson's *Dashing Wave* (FM 137), Dick Gray's *Godild* (R 98), Alfred 'Tub' Shrubsall's *Seven Brothers* (R 74)*, Tom Letley's *Magnet* (R 300), Harry Letley's *Providence* (R 225), Richard Shrubsall's *Jessie* (R 357) and the little clinker-built *Favourite* (R 105).

The pink shrimps, or 'Margate humps' as they were called, were much in demand during the summer season so of course the shrimp trawling boats needed to be based close to both the area where they could be found and the principal market. In the early years Medway and Swale bawleymen came down just for the summer shrimping and either laid up in the winter or went back home to go stowboating for whitebait and sprats or dredging for five-fingers that were sold to the farmers for manure. The prices of shrimps, cooked and ready for market, ranged from 1/- (5p) to 2/6 (12½p) a gallon. Occasionally they were sent up to the London market in grape barrels obtained from the greengrocers but often, after the freight charges had been met, the fishermen made only a shilling or two on each barrel.

The usual beam shrimp trawls were used, with a ground rope having a length of about one and a half times the beam and formed by wrapping old netting round a 3in rope and serving and rounding overall with lengths of old 2½in ropes, additional weight being provided by the sand and mud which got trapped inside. The rope core of the ground rope was spliced in the middle with only one tuck taken each side and seized. In the event of 'coming fast', the ground rope would then part before the trawl warp.

The Margate bawleys were unique in carrying a standing lug mizzen – like the luggers which were at this fishing station before the bawleys

* Later registered as LO 46 when owned by Bill Sutherland at Gravesend.

Another view from the Pier at about the same period. The nearest bawley (300 R) is *Magnet* and astern is *Mary* showing her later Faversham registration, FM 113.

arrived. The old registers indicate that bawleys were working from Margate as far back as 1869 when Wallace Shrubsall is shown as owner of the 'balley' *Brilliant* (R 64).She was an eight-ton craft with a keel length of 30ft. By 1874, the nine-ton *Star* (R 308) appears and the Milton fisherman Ben Redshaw's *Mary* was registered in the Ramsgate list in 1889. Also, as a result of the researches of Roger Letley into his family history, we know that in the early 1880s the three sons of Henry Letley of Arden Street, Gillingham (two of them already married) moved with their boats to Margate.

A descendant of one of these young men, Henry William Letley, grandson of the one with the same name, wrote from retirement at Oxford: 'Margate sandbanks several miles off the coast could at low tide cause a considerable diversion. If the wind was right and there was just enough water my grandfather knew where and when he could cross by doing what he called "two bumps and over". He would sail straight at the sand bar and bump the stem up on the ridge, the second wave would lift the bow and land the stern on the ridge, and then she would be over!'

Each bawley carried a crew of three: the skipper-owner, mate, and third hand; and each had the usual equipment including hand capstans and coal-fired coppers for boiling the shrimps. One of the largest of the fleet was probably *Magnet* (R 300) and she was one of the last to remain at Margate, always prominent with her untanned mainsail. The *Jessie* was of a similar size. Her owner, Richard Shrubsall, was a man of strong religious convictions. He would never sail on a Sunday and even if they went away on a Friday night's tide and became becalmed so that they could not make Margate by midnight on Saturday, he would lay-to all Sunday right up to midnight before heading for home. He had a trembling right hand due, it is said, to nerve damage sustained one day

Opposite: Margate Harbour in 1908 with the bawley fleet at moorings. Nearest the camera is a visiting bawley since she carries no mizzen mast. Beyond her are *Favourite* (F 105) and *Mary* (R 86). The sailing barge is probably unloading coal; her flag reads 'Margate Hoy Company'.

Some of the Margate fishermen and boatmen c.1925. Back to the camera is Teddy Parker and kneeling in the boat is 'Kitty' Hyde. (R. Munday)

The crew of *Moss Rose.* Left to right Arthur Mackie, Alfred Jones, William Mackie (father of Arthur), Steve Clayson and Johnny Cook. (D. Paterson)

when throwing a rope up to the pier. Oddly enough when he was net-making his hand would be as steady as a rock.

*Providence* (R 225) with dimensions of 37.5ft by 10.5ft by 4.3ft interior depth and 13.41 tons, was by about 1930 the last bawley to remain at the port. Henry William Letley had her built by S. Taylor of Milton Creek and delivered in February 1906. After his death in 1924 she was sold to his brother, Thomas William Letley, who had previously owned *Magnet*. After his death in 1928 the *Providence* was sold for £100 including all the gear to Mr Parker, owner of a fishmonger's shop in the town.

Motors were not installed until the very last days of the little fleet: they were frowned upon at first as it was thought that the fumes would taint the shrimps, and also because of the fire risk from the copper grate. Mr Parker had a Thorneycroft 8hp single-cylinder Handybilly engine installed in *Providence* by the local boat-builder, L.C. Brockman of Fort Mount. This performed satisfactorily and shortly afterwards her old topmast was removed and replaced with a neat stump topmast.

The *Providence* was well known as a very good sailer in light airs and could make three hauls to *Jessie*'s two in the right conditions, although the latter was a stiffer boat in a strong breeze.

In the 1930s, whilst owned by Mr Parker, *Providence* was worked by Paddy Walker and it was during this period that I especially remember her. 'Shipshape' really was the word for her; always beautifully maintained at a time when every penny counted. She made such an inspiring and colourful sight that many years ago I made a model of her, painted as I remembered her in all her glory, and the model eventually went to the fishing section of the National Maritime Museum (along with another model I built of the Brixham trawler *Valerian*).

*Providence* kept her little Handybilly engine and most of her sails right up to World War II. By 1946 however she had been fitted with a much larger Kelvin engine and powered capstan and had only a leg o'mutton trysail hooped to the old mainmast. She was then being used by Ben Frost and his brother-in-law, Ron Stephenson, for trawling and herring fishing, but on Ben's untimely death *Providence* was sold away in early 1950, thus ending the connection between Margate and bawley boats. By 1948 even the leg o'mutton trysail had been abandoned, with some unfortunate results. In July of that year *Providence* left Margate for a fishing trip at three o'clock in the morning, the crew accidentally breaking their water bottle shortly after leaving harbour. On reaching the fishing grounds about 16 miles out and getting the trawl shot the engine broke down. The old hand capstan had been replaced with a powered one operated from the main engine so the gear had to be manhandled aboard again. They tried for some five hours to get the engine going again but eventually a distress signal was hoisted. This was not seen so flares were burned as soon as it got dark.

Meanwhile the Margate lifeboat had been launched when it was realised that *Providence* was overdue. The flares guided the rescuers and the bawley was taken in tow for home at about 12.30am the following day, the crew having been without food or water for nearly 24 hours by the time they got back.

*Moss Rose* with some Edwardian trippers enjoying a sail. (D. Paterson)

*Moss Rose*, this time heavily overloaded with passengers and showing her forefoot in a lively swell. (D. Paterson)

## *Herring Punts*

The Margate herring punts were simply open clinker beach boats with transom stern and wash strake and capping about 8in high to provide freeboard. They went drifting for herring and sprats in the autumn and winter and were occasionally used for 'tripping', taking holidaymakers for sea trips in the summer.

The winter drifting rig was that of the traditional two-masted lugger: dipping lug mainsail and a standing lug mizzen with its clew sheeted to a long outrigger. In the summer they often carried a bawley-type loose-footed gaff mainsail with a single brail rope, but keeping the standing lugsail on the mizzen mast. A jib was set on the reefing bowsprit.

The Margate punts were very similar to the Deal foresail and mizzen punts which were used for the same kind of fishing, but the Deal boats did not have the iron horse across the stern for the sheet of the summer mainsail as carried by some of the Margate punts.

Among those remembered were *Britannia, British Lion* (R 186), Bob Ladd's *Grace Darling* (R 195), Charles 'Dusty' Miller's *Peep o'Day* (R 72), Walter Miller's *Edith Mary* (R 179) and Chris Case's *Enchantress* (R 97), these last two being owned at Westgate-on-Sea but worked out of Margate Harbour for the fishing season. The *Enchantress* was built in 1897 and survived at Westgate until 1947. She was 17.5ft by 6ft with an internal depth of 3.5ft and registered at 1.75 tons.

The *Edith Mary* was a typical example of a Margate herring punt and I am pleased that I thought to measure her and take some photographs before she finally fell to pieces in the early 1950s. She was built by William Henry Huggett, a Margate boatbuilder, in 1882 for Walter Miller of Westgate and was later taken over by his son, William Miller. She was built of oak and elm, having a length of 17ft 2in and a beam of 5ft 10in, the width of the transom being 3ft 4in and the depth from keel to top of transom was 3ft 10½in. There were three thwarts and below these in the middle of the boat the sides were ceiled from bilge to rising to provide a smooth internal surface to hold the pile of delicate cotton nets. Her eleven clinker strakes were fastened to 34 timbers each side.

Only the mizzen mast remained when I took these measurements, which incidentally differ a little from those shown in the Fishing Boat Register. The mizzen mast was 10ft 4in overall with a diameter of 2¾in, stepped just inside the transom slightly to starboard of the centre line, the sail sheeted to an outrigger that ran out through an opening in the transom alongside. The iron tiller passed through the offset slot in the transom and was kinked into a U-shape at the right point so that it would clear the mizzen mast when the helm was pushed to starboard.

The colour schemes were generally traditional. Outside the hull was tarred or black varnished below waterline. The topsides were clear varnished up to the rubbing strake which was black, as was the washstrake, with a white line along the bottom edge. The gunwale capping was usually grained along with the remainder of the gunwale.

Inside, the punts were usually black to the turn of the bilge, light stone colour from there to the risings, comb-grained and varnished from risings to gunwale and painted light stone colour again inside the deep

Whitehead's ticket office and chandlery in the 1920s. (D. Paterson)

A Margate herring punt with her dipping lugsail pulling well and showing her lug mizzen clewed to the long outrigger. She appears to be racing in a regatta.

washstrake. Bill Miller always took a great pride in the graining and added a bit of fancy figuring to good effect with the aid of a piece of potato. The light stone undercoat also formed the base colour for the scumble stain used for the graining. I remember some of the punts had the rounded moulding on the underside of the gunwale painted vermilion, which looked effective against the brown graining.

The *Edith Mary* figured in a hair-raising incident during the winter of 1938 when Bill Miller and Leslie Manning were out herring drifting about three-quarters of a mile off the Nayland Rock, Margate. They had a full fleet of fourteen nets out, three fathoms deep, and were waiting to haul. Suddenly an enormous tail erupted out of the water about thirty yards away and threshed about for several minutes causing a terrific shower of spray. It was in fact a thresher shark, which eventually broke through the nets after doing a great deal of damage and was not seen again.

## *Tripping*

After the advent of holidays by the sea in Victorian times, 'tripping' was an important part of the inshore fisherman's living. Margate and Ramsgate were for several generations a mecca for Londoners and sixty years ago one of the features of the holiday season at these resorts was the tripping yachts. A guidebook to Ramsgate of 1900 reads: 'Few visitors to Ramsgate miss the opportunity of indulging in a sea trip by one of the pleasure yachts manned by the sturdy seamen and storm warriors of the port. Moonlight excursions are popular and occasionally passengers are afforded the thrilling experience of landing on the dry Goodwin Sands from the vessels at low tide.' The word yacht tends to conjure up a picture of the plank-on-edge, narrow-gutted and rather lightly-built craft of the period, but such was not the case with the fine seaworthy craft that plied this trade in sailing days.

Back in the 1880s the *Royal Alfred* and *Cambria* were well known boats at Margate, and in 1890 the most famous of them all, *Moss Rose*, was launched. Built to the design of Mr E.S. Whitehead and strongly influenced by the bawleys, she was distinguished by having a most unusual launching. She measured 52.9ft in length by 17.5ft beam with a depth of 7.1ft and was of 34.79 registered tons. Built in a field by W.H. Huggett, she had to be transported to the harbour on a large trolley. Although the axles had been well greased, the friction produced by such a weight made them overheat and so *Moss Rose* proceeded on her way accompanied by a throng of men and boys throwing buckets of water over the bearings to keep them cool. She was being towed by a steam road-roller but after a while this broke down and the job was completed in a unique way. Lord John Sanger of circus fame (later to be murdered at Finchley and buried at Margate) loaned his team of elephants to complete *Moss Rose*'s journey to the harbour, Mr Whitehead distributing bags of nuts to the children to mark this auspicious event. Her success was immediate and so encouraging that Mr Huggett built the *Sunbeam* in 1891 to run in opposition. This vessel which had dimensions of 60.3ft by 18ft by 7.4ft internal depth, was fitted with a hand capstan and Jimmy

Margate Harbour around the turn of the century showing a number of luggers and wherries — the bawley fleet could have been out fishing. The hotel to the left is 'Stevens Hoy Hotel'.
(Kent County Council Library, Local Studies Dept)

The Margate bawley fleet sailing in company offshore. This photograph was taken from Margate Pier just before the First World War. (D. Paterson)

Oxley her skipper took her trawling in the North Sea during the winters. She was registered as R 137, a first class 43.23 tons fishing vessel, between the years 1895 and 1898, and after that was employed purely as a pleasure boat, but she was eventually sold, leaving the *Moss Rose* to have the cream of the tripping trade.

By this time the *Moss Rose* had grown in length. When first launched she had a yawl rig and transom stern, but Collar & Sons at Whitstable fitted her with an additional lute or false stern, so popular with the South Coast boats of the period, and she thus became ketch rigged and measured 55.5ft in length. This gave her more deck space and also improved her weatherly qualities by giving her more lift in a following sea. Her Board of Trade certificate gave her permission to carry 145 passengers, but she was known to have carried 200 when she was last boat away from *HMS Bulwark* which visited the town in 1906. Mr Whitehead owned her in partnership with Mr William Mackie and they ran her without a serious mishap for more than 30 years. She never did any trawling but among her more unusual jobs was a charter by Sir Richard Treves, physician to King Edward VII, to transport some valuable pictures to France.

On one occasion a little girl fell overboard and her father, who could not swim, immediately jumped in after her. Bill Mackie then dived in to rescue them both and for this he was awarded the Royal Humane Society's medal for saving life at sea. Later Bill Mackie himself fell overboard and was in turn rescued by Mr Whitehead, which took some living down.

In rig, *Moss Rose* closely resembled the bawleys, with her loose-footed mainsail and brail with the typical bawley mainsheet arrangement. She had a reefing bowsprit and her topmast could be housed, being fitted with a fid, all typical bawley features.

When the season was over *Moss Rose* was laid up each year at Harty Ferry in the Swale, as Margate Harbour is open to the north west and her usual mooring near the entrance was not safe in winter. Eventually she succumbed to the competition of the motor boat and was laid up in Ramsgate Harbour. She remained there until after World War II when she was bought by Sea Scouts and towed up to Plucks Gutter on the River Stour where her hulk remained for many years.

Mr Whitehead could be called the father of the pleasure boat trade at Margate. He was in partnership with Mr Bob Holness in the *Royal Alfred* and owned the *Cambria* before he was managing owner of the *Moss Rose*. One of those colourful personalities of his time, he never went to school for in those days practical experience was thought to be the finest possible training for a young man. In March 1870, when under 12 years of age, he was apprenticed on a Ramsgate smack but after a short time he ran away to join the deep water ships before finally settling down. He was second coxswain of the lifeboat *Quiver* and was awarded the Board of Trade Silver Medal for his part in the rescue of the crew of the brigantine *Druid* in November 1893.

When his seafaring days were over, Mr Whitehead kept a chandler's shop and travellers' ticket office in Cliftonville. I was only a boy at the

*Sunbeam* taking trippers aboard from Margate Jetty in the days when she competed with *Moss Rose*. The circular object hanging over her transom could have been a drogue (sea anchor).

time but remember the shop so well. How different from today's travel agents. Outside the shop stood a sign which read 'Ticket Office for Canada, America, India and the East'. In the window were coils of rope, blocks, deadeyes and other items of ship chandlery so that you felt that surely here was one travel office that really knew its business, not only booking the passage but able to fit out the ship as well! Here was another of those features of a bygone age at Margate that has gone for ever; like the thrill of sailing out close to the lightship to throw newspapers, books and cigarettes on board, and the moonlight trips and musical evenings of those unsophisticated days.

## *Pole trucks*

Before leaving this chapter a few words should be said about the unique pole trucks used for moving wherries and sometimes herring punts over the sands. The trolley wheels were of the traditional iron-tyred cartwheel type of about 4ft 6in across and they were joined by a wrought iron cranked axle fitted with a hook each side. In the centre of the cranked axle was a stayed wooden beam of about 10ft in length. To lift the wherry the trolley was pushed right over the top of the boat until the hooks were near the known point of balance of the boat. The beam was then tipped up so that the rear end at the cranked axle sank down and a served chain could be passed under the boat's keel and attached at each side to the hooks forged on the axle. The forward end of the trolley beam was then brought down thus levering the boat clear of the sand. The forward end of the beam was lashed down to the wherry's bow ring and the pole truck could be pushed across the beach. The large diameter wheels did not dig too deeply into the sand and the spokes were helpful in the general pushing and manhandling. To lower the wherry again the bow lashing was cast off and the beam tipped up, so lowering the boat, and when the chain strop was unhooked the job was done. We may never know how this simple device evolved, but it was entirely right for moving small boats across Thanet's sandy foreshore.

A model of the Broadstairs herring punt *Invicta* donated to the Science Museum by Edgar J. March. Launched in 1883, *Invicta* fished for herring and sprats in autumn and winter and took visitors for pleasure trips in summer. The model shows the punt in summer rig of loose-footed mainsail on a gaff 12ft long, the standing lug mizzen has a yard 6ft long and an out-rigger 8.75ft long. The mainmast was 22.75ft high, the mizzen mast 11.75ft and the bowsprit 12ft long (6.75ft outboard). In winter the reduced rig was carried on a mainmast of 16.25ft and a mizzen of 10.5ft. The boat's length was 19ft overall with a beam of 6.5ft. Other sails included a staysail, large jib and spinnaker or balloon jib. (Science Museum)

The Margate herring punt *Edith Mary* (R 179) at the end of her days around 1950. A pole truck wheel can be seen on the right. (D. Paterson)

# 10

# *Thanet Round to Broadstairs*

It was not just a matter of artists' licence that, in times past, illustrations of the Kentish shore managed to include one or two open boats pulled up on almost every stretch of beach. There were in fact many such little boats and they were used in season for the herring, mackerel and sprat harvest by men who at other times worked mainly on the land. Edgar March quotes from a book written in 1723 by the Rev. John Lewis, Vicar of Minster, which describes how farm labourers bargained with their employers to go on the 'shot-fare' and 'herring-fare'. Shot-fare was the mackerel fishing season in May, after barley-sowing, and herring-fare fitted in after the harvest but before November when the wheat had to be sown. The men, he said, were equally adept at plough and tiller.

Herring drifting from small boats is still carried on from Margate harbour, the experience of the older men having been passed on to the younger generation despite the interval of some years when herring fishing was very poor and then banned to conserve stocks. The motor boats used now still do much the same job as the clinker herring punts and rowing wherries in the first sixty or so years of the century. Don Paterson describes in his chapter on Margate the smart little herring punts of 16 to 20ft. The wherries were rowing skiffs of 17ft or so, similar in general form to those still to be seen, in lighter construction, on the Upper Thames and other English rivers.

The wherries were familiar boats to generations of Margate holidaymakers, being worked for hire or short trips from the harbour slipway or alongside the jetty, and when not in use were brought ashore on pole trucks. Most of the wherries were built locally, towards the end by W.H. Huggett, or by L.C. Brockman, whose old yard can still be seen at Fort Mount.

The wherries were sometimes used for drifting, but mainly for beating, a kind of peter-netting described later, or for lobstering 'off the rocks' just offshore. Much of the catch was sold by Margate boatmen to local people at the harbour, as it still is, and Tom Redshaw told how in the 1920s the freshly caught herrings retailed nominally at 36 fish for 1/- (5p), but his father did not bother to count them out; he just slung a good load into each waiting bucket.

The punts were employed in fishing all round the East Kent coast and down as far as Dungeness. At Dover and Broadstairs, as well as Margate, punts were used in foying (supplying equipment and stores) to ships offshore, and also for tripping work during the summer season. Mackerel drifting was not such an important source of income at Margate as it was on the south coast of Kent where at Dungeness for instance the fishermen started drifting in early May and continued until July when the fish shoals were coming up Channel from the west, and the fishing resumed for another six weeks in the autumn as the fish worked their way back down Channel again. The cotton drift nets were dressed with linseed oil for herring and sprat fishing but could be cutched (tanned) for mackerel since this species could only be caught after dark, whereas herring and sprats were to be taken in daylight too if the water was cloudy.

The Thanet wherry was a long, narrow pulling boat, usually of pitch pine clinker strakes on oak timbers. There were three thwarts and side seats, the backboard to the after thwart normally carrying a handsome brass nameplate. They had yoke steering over a narrow transom which, set high over the skeg, allowed the boat to be beached by the stem while waves parted comfortably under the transom. Wherries often carried a dipping lugsail, but only sailed when the wind was free as the long keel prevented them winding without use of oars. The oars were straight chestnut sweeps worked in bronze crutches set in chocks outside the gunwale. Reckoned to be good little sea boats, the wherries were easy to row, both forwards and backwards. For short distances the boatman would usually row standing, facing the way he was going.

Vernon Kennard, who used the Margate wherry, *Haughty Belle,* up to 1978 before she went to the National Maritime Museum, is the source of much of the information here. He estimates that there could have been upwards of fifty Thanet wherries in use up to World War II, but only seven or eight afterwards. Many were requisitioned (with compensation) by the Navy just before Dunkirk, but some of these, after being towed out to a minesweeper anchored offshore, were carelessly lifted by davit tackle hooked to the wherries' thwarts and were too damaged to be put to further use. The most popular place for keeping wherries when not afloat was at Coldharbour, just to the east of Margate jetty, where a gap through the rocks allowed boats to be launched or recovered when the tide was down. Incidentally, Margate folk call their harbour jetty the pier: and the old pleasure pier, before it was destroyed, was known as the jetty.

Wherries were kept varnished (as long as the wood was sound) above the waterline outside, the bottoms black varnished. Inside was traditionally grained and if the wherry was used for pleasure hiring the thwarts and side seats were often upholstered. To finish off there was sometimes a white 'eye' painted at the stem and the truck of the mast was painted white also.

Alf Manning remembered that the wherries were hired out at 3/- (15p) an hour before the last War and in those better-mannered days people would listen to the boatman if he advised them for instance to go west towards Epple Bay so that they could return with wind and tide. Naturally if the boatman, on sizing up his prospective customers,

Margate Harbour with wherries on the slipway c.1930.

decided that they did not look competent to go out alone he would insist that they would have to be content with his taking them for the traditional 'long ride'. As Vernon Kennard said, the typical boatman that everyone pictures in memory now wore a flat cap, collarless shirt, waistcoat and rolled up trousers above bare feet.

Vernon was the final owner of *Joken,* a small wherry, or perhaps more accurately a skiff, of only about 15ft. He bought her from Bill Miller who was the last local boatman to give holidaymakers rowing trips from the beach, at St Mildred's Bay, Westgate-on-Sea. This ended sometime around 1974. *Joken* was believed to have been built by Brockman's apprentice, Jack Titcomb, in 1939. The surviving *Haughty Belle,* now in the care of the National Maritime Museum, measures 17ft 1in overall (16ft 2in inside) with a beam of 4ft 9in and internal depth of 1ft 8in. She was originally called *Blossom* but renamed after the first *Haughy Belle,* owned by 'Kitty' Hyde, was destroyed in the 1953 gales.

Charlie Miller had three wherries which he and Alf Manning hired out, *Royal Sovereign, Edith* and *Daisy Ellen.* Bill Miller had, besides *Joken,* the *Jezzamine* and *Moss Rose.* Ralph Turner went drifting for herring in *May-Florence* until about 1965 and Bert Munday and his old fishing partner Dick Morris used a wherry for the same purpose up to about 1970. She was *Silver Spray* built by Harry Brockman.

For decades wherries, like many other small boats around our coasts, were built for £1 per foot in length. Or, in this case, you could buy a wherry fully equipped with spars and lugsail for just £20.

Wherries were handy for lobstering, occasionally with the hinged hoopnets (called clapnets at Margate) or, more commonly, with special Thanet type pots. These were oblong shaped and collapsible for storage,

Vernon Kennard with his wherry *Haughty Belle* (ex *Blossom*) shortly before she left for the National Maritime Museum in 1978. (Bruce Searle, *Thanet Gazette*)

Vernon Kennard's skiff *Joken* on her pole truck at Kingsgate in 1960s.

and since they were generally known as Broadstairs pots they are more fully described later.

Crabs, which at Margate are known as 'pungers', were also liable to end up in the pots but were sometimes caught in a very different way. Ron Munday showed me his old pungering hook, the shaft of a golfing iron with the end cut off and the point sharpened and bent round in a hook. Most of his contemporaries had simply bent the end of a metal stair rod or something similar. They went pungering at low water, clambering over the rocks and hooking out the edible crabs from their holes under the fringes of seaweed.

Drift-netting for herring out of Margate and the neighbouring small bays continued, probably on much the same scale as it had in previous centuries, right up to about 1950, but declined thereafter. About thirty small boats from Margate harbour alone, mainly punts and wherries, went 'errin'in' every year in September and October. This was followed by spratting from November to January or February, the best catches made on bright moonlit nights. Fewer nets were used than for herring because the sprat shoals could be very dense.

Herring drift nets are usually 30 or 40 yards long by three fathoms in depth, and sprat nets only two fathoms deep. They were originally braided of cotton dressed with boiled linseed oil. After use they were simply hung up to dry and never tanned. Although latterly bought from Joseph Gundry's of Bridport they were also braided locally at one time, Wally Gibson being the last netmaker.

In Thanet herring drift nets are attached to their head ropes by individual lashings known as nossels (pronounced 'nozzles') and the lint (net itself) is set-in by the third, as the old term has it, so that the mesh hangs in a deep diamond shape. With other types of wall net, such as the smelt dragnets on the Medway, the same result is achieved by stapling, that is to say by continuous lacing of yoke lines ('yorklins'). The other function of the nossels (sometimes called snoods) is to prevent the lint of the drift net rolling up on itself.

The old cotton drift nets did not have full ground ropes but short lengths of rope were sewn in along the bottom of the lint and these incorporated small lead weights. Generally, all natural fibre nets set better for being given a soaking in seawater before being shot, but this was not possible with the long fleets of herring and sprat drift nets at Thanet. Alf Manning noted that new nets were usually bought in spring or summer well before they needed to be used. They were well soaked in a drum of linseed oil and then put through the rubber rollers of a mangle to remove excess oil. After that the nets were spread out over a nearby field, of corn stubble for preference, and left for a few days to dry. Naturally no one touched them; the fishermen left them out with no fear of theft or vandalism.

The top 12 inches or so of herring nets are double-knit and this in the past was called scudding locally as well as the more usual name of heading. It is needed to support the weight of lint hanging below. The nets are suspended from floats (bobbers) by rope strops about 9ft long and these allow the net to be set at the desired depth below the surface.

Usually the headrope is at a depth of about a fathom but can be right up to the floats depending on the fisherman's judgment of the colour and clarity of the water: the clearer the water, the lower the net must be.

At Margate boats of up to about 20ft still work fleets of herring nets, all laced together end-to-end in a continuous line in the traditional way (as were the mackerel nets). Sprat nets by contrast were only laced together at the head and foot; they were also about 30 yards long and were worked in fleets of about nine for the punts and six for the wherries. The wherries, which could carry a maximum of eight or nine herring nets in a fleet might catch up to 2,000 fish in a night tide. Bert Munday described how he went overnight fishing with his partner in *Silver Spray,* leaving on the ebb and usually rowing down as far as Walpole Bay, then shooting the three fathom deep fleet of nets in about 3½ fathoms of water and so drifting quietly back with the young flood to Margate Harbour. The sailing punts reckoned to work fleets of around 15 herring nets, but no doubt, as always, there were variations to suit the individual strengths and inclinations of the men concerned.

To shoot herring drift nets in the days before motors the boat had to be propelled downwind and across tide, either by rowing or by using the mizzen sail in a herring punt, with the net being streamed from the bow. Finally the 40 fathom 'swing rope' was run out and the long wall of net stretched out, for nearly a third of a mile under the surface of the dark sea if the full fleet of 15 joined nets had been shot, and the boat then rode quietly head to wind.

Alf Manning described how, when he returned from minesweeping after World War II, he joined Dusty (Charles) Miller to work the punt *Peep O'Day* (R 72). Dusty had been working the boat throughout the war with an older partner but they were only permitted to fish during daylight hours. *Peep O'Day* was just over 16ft in length, gaff-rigged with two suits of sails. A smart white mainsail was set during the summer tripping season and a tanned (cutched) mainsail and older headsails during the autumn and winter fishing seasons.

On reaching the place where the net was to be shot the mainsail was dropped and the clew of the mizzen could be brought inboard from the outrigger bumpkin and held at the boat's quarter. This 'backpiping' enabled the punt to be sailed stern first across the tide as the nets were shot from the bow. The rudder was removed for this manoeuvre and the boat was steered with one of the 18ft oars over the stem. When the full fleet of nets and the swing rope had all been run out the boat's rudder was dropped back on its gudgeon and pintle and the mizzen sail let out again so that the punt would lie comfortably head to wind.

The swing rope had a swivel shackle at the net end and the boat end came in over the fairlead and was made fast to the samson post. In rough weather an iron 56lb weight was lashed to the swing rope to absorb the shocks of the boat snatching against the nets and thus pulling them out of shape which would have prevented the mesh gilling the fish. This was the traditional way of herring drifting which Alf Manning remembered continuing until about 1950. It is still possible to catch 40 or 50 stones (700lbs) of herring in a tide off Margate and up to 100 stones in a tide's

Broadstairs in the 1890s with luggers as well as punts in the harbour. (G. Strevens)

drifting off the North Foreland. But it is easier now with motor fishing boats: Alf recalled that in the old days after drifting the nine miles or so along the coast up to Reculver, as the tide turned the wind so often seemed inconsiderately to expire, and it was a long row home pulling on the punt's heavy 18ft oars.

Bert Munday told how he went beating with Richard Morris up till sometime around 1970 in the wherry *Silver Spray*, the only difference from the old days being that after World War II the use of trammel nets was general. The invoice for the last net they bought in 1960 from Joseph Gundry & Co. of Bridport already has a period tone. It cost nearly £30 and was 6ft deep and 60 fathoms in length. 'Inner Net ex 32/15 ply Cotton, 3in mesh, Standard Walls 18in mesh. Barked and fitted complete with lines, Corks and Leads. Ready for Sea.'

Sea bass were the prime quarry and on fine summer nights right up to the end of September they would row down with the ebb to Kingsgate Castle, then at low tide and working very quietly they shot the buoyed net in a fathom or so of water outside the rocks. When the net was in place the men beat the water with weighted poles 19ft long to drive the fish into the beat net. Apart from bass they had caught red mullet, soles, dogfish and even the occasional conger eel. Before the war sea trout were also sought but these are rare now.

Beating was also described to me by Harold Letley of Westgate whose grandfather was one of the three brothers who had moved to Margate from the Medway in about 1882. Harold's grandfather had had a 16ft punt *Hettie* built at Whitstable, mainly of elm. Harold's father, who had

Broadstairs Harbour around 1900 with a number of punts and wherries, the Fishermen's Boathouse on the right.

George Strevens taking trippers for the traditional 'long ride' aboard the wherry *Uncle George* c.1960. (G. Strevens)

at one time crewed with his uncle on the bawley *Providence*, gave up full-time fishing in about 1930 but had the 13ft *Helenus*, which is still stored ashore. She was probably the last boat built at Westgate, by a relative, Percy Letley, in about 1927. Both boats when beating would normally work the three or four miles along the coast from Minnis Bay to Epple Bay where they were based, beating in up to a fathom and a half of water just off the rocks. In those days a trammel net was not used so the normal corked and leaded seine type net of about 20 fathoms long was shot with buoys and anchors at each end, the down-tide end being brought in nearer to the rocks so that the net described a J-curve. After the net was down they rowed inshore of it and beat water to frighten the fish into the bight of the net. The net was hauled in the usual way, cork line and lead line together in the hands of the man standing in the stern, the net being flaked down in the stern sheets so that the catch and debris could be shaken out as the net was shot again. The catch was usually of flatties: plaice, soles and skate.

Broadstairs, like Margate, at one time had a fleet of sailing luggers, but by the early years of this century they had all gone, leaving only the smaller herring punts and the wherries as the transition to engined craft took place. In addition to the seasonal fishing, the punts were employed at hovelling: supplying stores and equipment to sailing vessels offshore. The Broadstairs men for a long period kept one standby boat on the ramp beside the Captain Digby public house for this job because, being just around the chalk headland, it was more sheltered for launching into southerly and south-westerly gales than the town's harbour.

The lovely old black-tarred pier which juts out so sturdily into the sea at the north end of Main Bay to provide a haven for small craft dates back to 1538 and it carries a venerable weather-boarded fishermen's boathouse complete with two figureheads. The whole is redolent of Broadstairs' lively maritime history; no wonder that Charles Dickens loved this small fishing station which yet manned an important sailing and pulling lifeboat into this century. It was of course the proximity of the Goodwins that made a lifeboat so essential here. Salvaging was in the blood. Even up to the first year or two of World War II the Broadstairs boatmen could not resist a quiet foray out to a mined cargo ship that had fetched up on those notorious sands. Before that, in the early 1930s, Edward 'Porky' Croom managed to tow in a disabled foreign schooner with a cargo of dried cod from near the North Goodwins light vessel to Dover Harbour. He had a house built largely on the salvage proceeds and gratefully named it after the schooner, the *Gifeon*.

Most small fishing stations around our coast were dominated by two or three fishing families and at Broadstairs it was the Crooms and Hillers. George Strevens, who was born and raised at the nearby hamlet of Reading Street, had to start his fishing by going to Margate for the herring drifting, working with Bob and Arthur Ladd in their punt *Grace Darling*. In the 1930s herring were sold to the public at around 1/- (5p) for 40, and on Saturday evenings the customers could practically take as many as they wanted because the fish would not keep until Monday and no marketing was allowed on Sundays, except for mackerel.

The old launching ramp through an opened cave in the chalk cliffs beside the Captain Digby public house, Kingsgate c.1930. The wherry on the left is probably Dick Miller's *Sunbeam* and the skiff on the right appears to be the *Brentwood*.

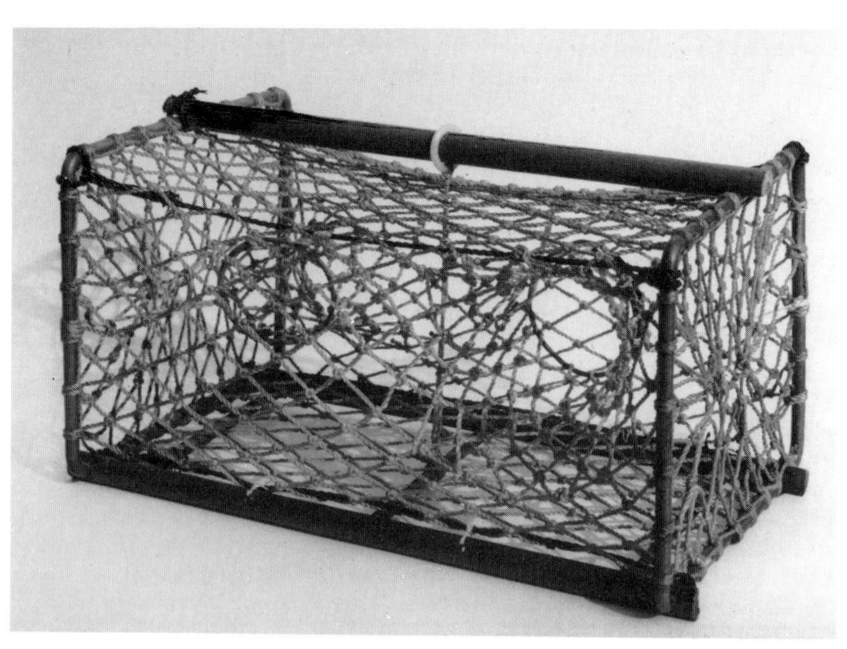

Model of a Broadstairs collapsible lobster or crab pot, as described in the text. The two apertures, one on each side, can be seen in the photograph, with the bait string rising from the centre of the pot's base to the middle of the wooden stretcher on top. (G. Strevens)

Between the wars the Broadstairs men mainly went after herring in the autumn and early winter (they reckoned the peak of the season was Guy Fawkes' Day) and lobsters from about Easter until September. There was also a shorter crabbing season from just before Easter until May. It was traditional to start potting during the week preceding Easter, whenever that fell, so that the local hotels could be supplied with shellfish when the first holiday visitors arrived. The fishermen received 1/- per lb for lobsters but 2/6 (12½p) for exceptionally large ones.

For both crabs and lobsters, the Broadstairs rectangular oblong folding pot was invariably used; at least within living memory which roughly embraces the period since World War I. The need for this space-saving device may have arisen from the limited capacity of the herring punts which the men used to tend and service the 80 pots each that was customary. The pots folded flat and could be stacked when being transported, although there was still the 10 fathoms of rope and a marker buoy for each pot to stow.

The pots were originally made with a wooden frame about 3ft long by 1ft 6in wide, often from pieces of broken deckchair. The iron or steel end frames ('hoops') were bent into the rectangular shape, folding inwards when the pot was collapsed. This framework enclosed the netting which was braided in a tube of 32 meshes laced up at each end. There was an aperture on each side, from which led inwards short funnels of net ending in iron rings suspended by bracing cords above the bait. The main tube of net was pulled into the oblong shape of the frame by four lengthwise pieces of cord stretched tightly to each corner, and it was against this tension that the wooden stretcher kept the upright hoops vertical and the whole pot rigid, one hoop being lashed to the stretcher and the other forced into a large notch at the end. Durability was improved by dipping the pot in a tar tank kept handy for the purpose. The wooden pots were heavily ballasted, often with two seven pound window sash weights, to keep them on the seabed. After World War II six-foot lengths of ex-Army angle iron became available so the fishermen switched to these for the base frame of their pots and no other weight was then needed. The bait was held in the centre of the pot on a double cord attached to a cross piece on the base and running up through the top of the net and made fast to the stretcher. The bait was held against the bottom knot on the cord (about 3in above the base) by either a sliding knot or by a piece of leather threaded on the bait cords. Mackerel was reckoned to be the best bait, but did not hold on the cord well so either two or four heads of plaice were commonly used. They were nicked with a knife each side to hold between the bait cords more firmly; and by tradition there had to be a white (underside) of fish head at both top and bottom of the pile to attract the shellfish. Usually the trapped lobsters or crabs could be grabbed and brought out of the pot by the fisherman reaching inside through one of the entrance tubes, but a very large specimen might need one end of the net tube unlaced.

Each boat managed about 80 pots, every pot being buoyed separately on 10 fathoms of rope, this being divided into seven fathoms of good new rope fastened at the lower end to the pot and with an eye splice at

Although perhaps outside the scope of this book, it is worth showing this photograph to prove that bawleys worked from Ramsgate in the first two or three decades of this century. The bawley with sails hoisted is R 235, *Brunette*, owned by Charles Wells (registered in 1906 at 5.14 tons with dimensions of 34ft by 11.2ft; broken up 1920). (National Maritime Museum)

the upper end to which was attached by a sheet bend three fathoms of older rope. This was the length that attracted weed ('grass') since it was on or near the surface at low tide, and this section was frequently replaced and taken ashore to be dried off and cleaned.

At Broadstairs the wherries were used almost entirely for holiday tripping. George Strevens had *Seaflower* but changed her name to *Uncle George*. He remembered that the largest wherry, *Irex*, belonged to 'Shar' Hiller and measured about 18ft 10in by 5ft (compared with the normal 18ft length and 4ft 9in beam or thereabouts). Most of the wherries had come from Brockman's yard in latter years (although *Seaflower* and a number of others had been built at Ramsgate around 1953). They were kept well varnished on topsides, with tarred bottoms inside and out, but above the bottom boards inside up to the rising was often painted, frequently a light blue colour.

The boatman could sit on the bow of his wherry keeping her grounded on the sands while the fine stern was afloat and neatly parting the waves so that she did not tend to broach to. A maximum of eight persons was supposed to be carried and the charge was 1/- (5p) for adults and 6d (2½p) for children. The traditional 'long ride' lasted about 10 minutes and usually took the holidaymakers southwards (inshore to dodge the prevailing tide flow) from Main Bay to Louisa Bay, then out round Beacon Rock, back offshore with the tide to the pierhead and thence to the sands again.

# *Select Bibliography*

Benham, Hervey – *Last Stronghold of Sail* (George G. Harrap & Co), *Once Upon a Tide* (George G. Harrap & Co), *The Stowboaters* (Essex County Nespapers 1977)

Carr, Frank – *Vanishing Craft* (Country Life 1934)

Clark, Roy – *The Longshoremen* (David & Charles 1974)

Collard, Allan O. – *The Oyster and Dredgers of Whitstable* (Joseph Collard 1902)

Davis, F.M. – *An Account of the Fishing Gear of England & Wales* (HMSO 1958)

Goodsall, Robert H. – *Whitstable, Seasalter and Swalecliffe* (Cross & Jackman, Canterbury 1938)

Hillier, Caroline – *The Bulwark Shore* (Granada 1980)

Leather, John – *Gaff Rig* (Adlard Coles/Granada Publishing 1970)

March, Edgar J. – *Inshore Craft of Britain in the Days of Sail and Oar* (David & Charles 1970)

Murie, Dr James – *Kent and Essex Sea Fisheries Committee: Report of the Sea Fisheries and Fishing Industries of the Thames Estuary* (Waterlow Bros 1903)

Simper, Robert – *Beach Boats of Britain* (The Boydell Press, Woodbridge 1984)

Stevens, J.E. – *Whitstable Natives* (Hartley Reproductions, New Ash Green, Dartford, Kent)

Stibbons, Lee and Warren – *Crabs and Shannocks: The Longshore Fishermen of North Norfolk* (Poppyland Publishing, Cromer 1983)

Winstanley, Michael J. –*Life in Kent at the Turn of the Century* (Wm Dawson & Son, Folkestone 1978)

Wyllie, W.L. and Mrs – *London to the Nore* (A & C Black 1905)

# *Glossary of Nautical Terms*

A'weather – towards windward side.
Beat (verb) – to sail to windward on zigzag course.
Bend (verb) – to fasten, generally with rope.
Bight – loop in a rope; also bend in a river.
Bilge – turn of boat's hull section where topsides meet bottom planks; also space below floorboards.
Bill – tip of anchor fluke (q v).
Bitts – upright posts or timber heads projecting above deck.
Block – pulley.
Bobstay – stay leading from outboard end of bowsprit downwards to stem of boat.
Bower – main (bow) anchor.
Bowline – loop tied in rope; also short rope for securing purposes.
Bowse (verb) – to haul down taut.
Bowsprit – spar projecting from bow to allow vessel to set jib.
Brail – rope which runs on both sides of the mainsail of bawleys and dobles (also barges) used for gathering in the sail to mast.
Bullseye block – round hardwood thimble (q v).
Carvel – strakes (planks) on side and bottom of boat which are set flush, not overlapped.
Chainplates – metal straps on boat's topsides to which the shrouds are attached.
Cheek – shoulder of wood projecting from masthead or a spar.
Clench (verb) – to secure strakes clinker fashion with rivets or nails.
Clew – lower, after corner of fore and aft sail.
Clinker (or clincher) – strakes which overlap.
Coaming – rail around the edge of hold or hatchway.
Cod-end – closed (tied) end of trawl net.
Covering board – outer plank of deck covering the heads of vessel's frames.
Cranse iron – iron ring with lugs for rigging at outboard end of bowsprit.
Cringle – rope eye formed in bolt rope of sail enclosing a thimble (q v).
Crosstrees – struts of wood or iron at masthead to allow tensioning of topmast shrouds.
Cutch – extract of foreign tree bark (acacia catechu) formerly sold in blocks and used for tanning sails and nets.

Dagger board – drop-keel raised and lowered through bottom of boat.
Deadeyes – thick discs of hardwood with sheaveless holes through which lanyards are rove to set up rigging.
Dipping lug – lugsail which has to be lowered and moved to the other side of the mast on each tack when beating to windward.
Downhaul – rope by which a sail is hauled down.
Fairlead – eye, fitting or hole to guide rope.
Fid – removable pin at heel of topmast, also pin through inboard end of bowsprit.
Flake (verb) – to lay out net or rope in layers, free of snarls so that it will run clear.
Fleet (verb) – to ease rope or chain around windlass etc.
Fluke – flattened hook at end of anchor arm; also old name for flatfish.
Forepeak – space immediately aft of boat's stem.
Foresail – (on a cutter) the triangular sail set from forestay.
Forestay – stay leading from stem to masthead.
Foying (verb) – see hovelling.
Gaff – spar from which four-sided fore and aft sail is suspended eg mainsail on a cutter.
Gammon iron – ring at stem of boat through which bowsprit passes.
Garboard – the strake of planking immediately above the keel.
Grommet – a ring of rope.
Halyard – rope for hoisting sails, gaff or flag.
Hatchboat – spritsail rigged craft with wet well.
Horse – iron bar running across deck to which is attached the sheets of fore and aft sails.
Hounds – alternative word for cheeks.
Hovelling (verb) – supplying stores and equipment (eg replacement anchors) to ships offshore.
Hufflers – men plying for hire to assist bargemen by raising and lowering masts when shooting bridges.
Jackline – rope holding jib-headed topsail to topmast (instead of mast hoops).
Jib – triangular headsail which on a cutter is generally set from masthead to bowsprit.
Jib-headed – sail in the shape of a jib.
Keel sail – old sail hung weighted below the water to harness the force of the tide.
Keelson – timber inside boat's hull lying along length of keel proper.
Knightheads – posts supporting bowsprit at the stem of a vessel.
Leech – after edge of fore and aft sail.
Lint – netting, especially in wall nets.
Luff – forward edge of fore and aft sail.
Luff up (verb) – to bring boat closer into the wind.
Lugsail – four-sided sail attached to yard which is slung to mast part of the way along the yard.
Lute stern – overhang built on transom to give lift in following sea (from shape of stern elevation).
Marline – twine composed of two strands.

Mizzen – smaller, after mast; also the sail set on the mizzen mast.
Nettles – small lines used for various lashings, often of ropeyarns.
Outhaul – rope which hauls sail out eg the jib along bowsprit.
Outrigger – boomkin (or bumkin) projecting from stern of herring punt to hold the clew of mizzen sail abaft the transom.
Parbuckle (verb) – to lift or lower an object by passing rope round to obtain purchase.
Parcel (verb) – to wind strips of material round rope.
Peak – uppermost part of gaff sail.
Pole – (of mast) the upper end of mast above rigging.
Pole mast – lower mast and topmast in one piece.

Reach (verb) – to sail with wind on boat's side.
Reef (verb) – to shorten sail; also to partly run in bowsprit.

Reeve (verb) – to pass rope through aperture. Past tense: rove.
Risings – horizontal strips of wood which support boat's thwarts.
Roove – collar placed over copper nail before clenching.
Ruck (verb) – to drop peak of mainsail, as when scandalising.
Sailing beam – deck beam of boat adjacent to mast (the principal beam).
Sampson post – strong post forward for making fast anchor chain, drift net etc.
Scandalise (verb) – to reduce working area of mainsail by tricing up the tack and/or lowering the peak.
Scantlings – dimensions of boat's timbers.
Scarf (verb) – to join timbers by tapering the ends wedge fashion and fitting together.
Scuttle – opening in decks or cabin top to allow crew to go below.

Seize (verb) – to secure by lashing with cord etc.
Sheave – grooved wheel inside block or spar around which rope runs.
Sheet – rope controlling the clew of sail.
Shrouds – standing rigging from masthead to sides of boat to support mast.
Single whip – a tackle with one block.
Skiff – small open boat.
Snatchblock – block open at one end to allow rope to be applied to sheave without reeving through.
Spider band – metal hoop around base of mast fitted with cleats or belaying pins for making fast halyards etc.
Sprit – spar set diagonally from base of mast to peak of four-sided fore and aft sail.
Stanliff – rope tackle on a pendant attached to heel of sprit and providing support from masthead.
(in) Stays – going about, winding.
Strake – plank along side of vessel.

Sweeps – large oars; ropes at ends of dragnets.
Surge (verb) – to ease rope round windlass etc.
Tack – forward lower corner of sail.
Tackle – purchase with block(s); general term for boat gear.
Thimble – metal or hardwood ring set in sail or spliced in rope.
Tholes – pegs fitted in gunwales for various purposes.
Thwart – seat set athwart (across) small boat.
Tilt – removable shelter of canvas or tarpaulin.
Topping lift – rope which takes the weight of a spar.
Transom – square stern (originally the beams to form this kind of stern).
Trice (verb) – to draw up tack of mainsail by means of line from masthead.
Truss (verb) – see trice.
Warp – rope used for mooring; rope used for towing beam trawl.
Washstrakes – uppermost planks of small boat above gunwale.
Wending – see winding.
Wet well – compartment in hull of boat perforated to allow water to flow through and so keep the catch fresh and preferably alive.
Winding (verb) – to put vessel on another tack when sailing against the wind.
Windlass – horizontal winch.
Wink – winch set on post amidships on some bawleys, used for hauling in trawl.
Yard topsail – four sided topsail with spar along head.

# *Lines & Sail Plans*

| | by courtesy of |
|---|---|
| *Thistle* (length 35′4″)<br>*Stormy Petrel* (length 40′3″) | H E (Ted) Penny,<br>C Eng, MRINA, MIMarE,<br>41 Castlemaine Avenue,<br>Gillingham, Kent, ME7 2QA<br>(Tel: Medway 571569) |
| *Rosa & Ada*<br>*Argonaut* | The Board of Trustees & Director,<br>Science Museum,<br>London, SW7 2DD |

'THISTLE'

MEDWAY BAWLEY

The lines of Medway bawley *Thistle* built by Gill's in 1887. (Ted Penny)

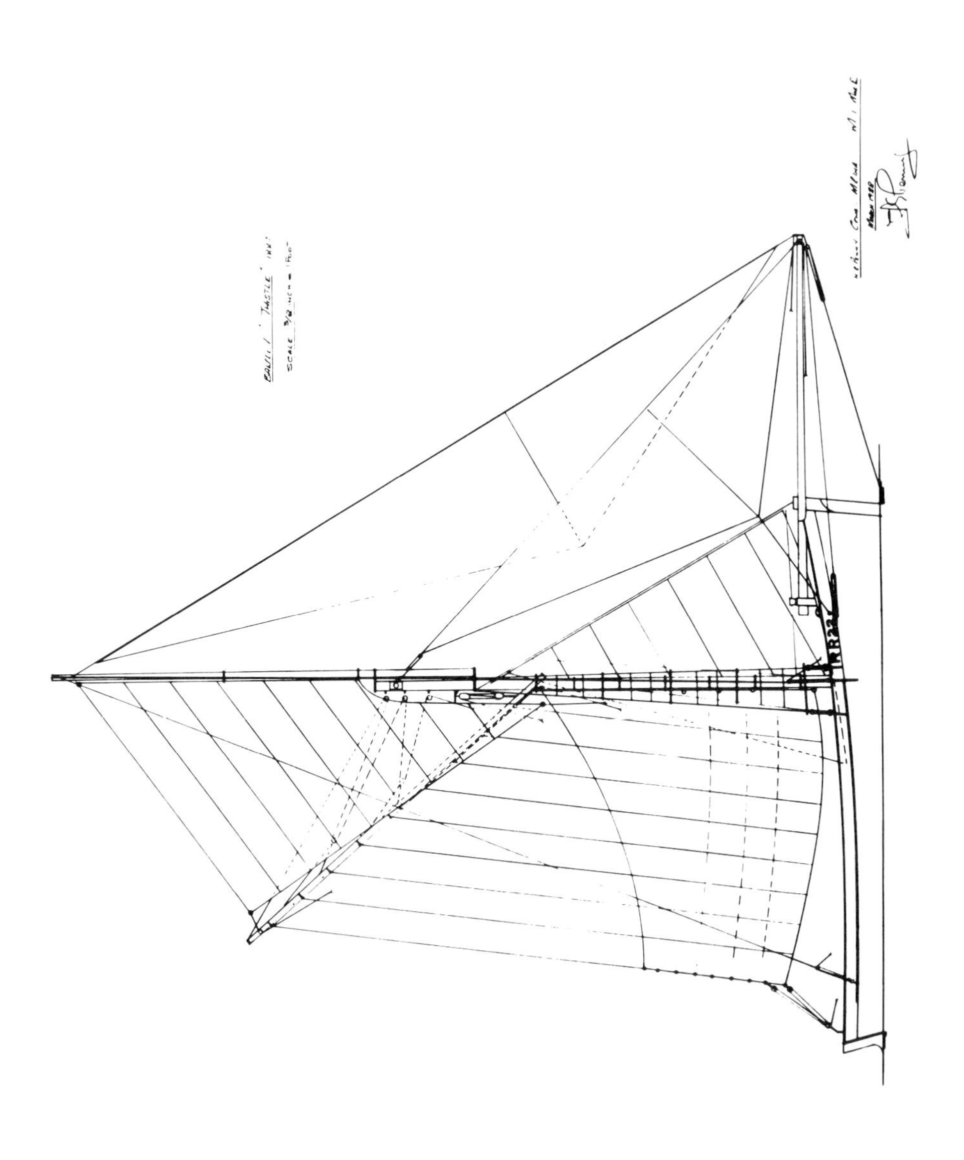

Sail plan of *Thistle*. The measurements are taken from a modern suit of sails and are not intended to indicate the original rig. (Ted Penny)

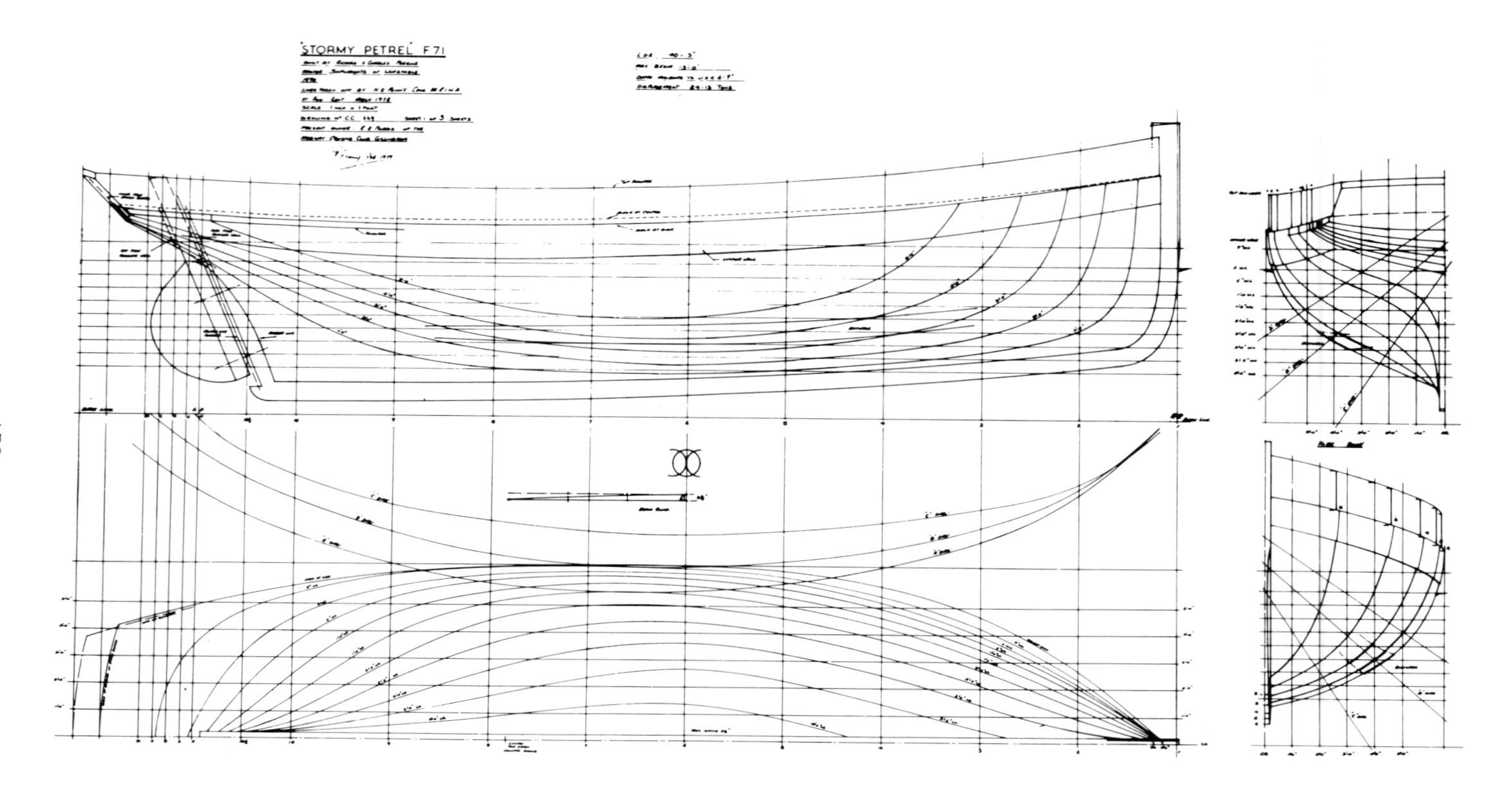


The lines of Whitstable smack *Stormy Petrel* built in 1890. (Ted Penny)

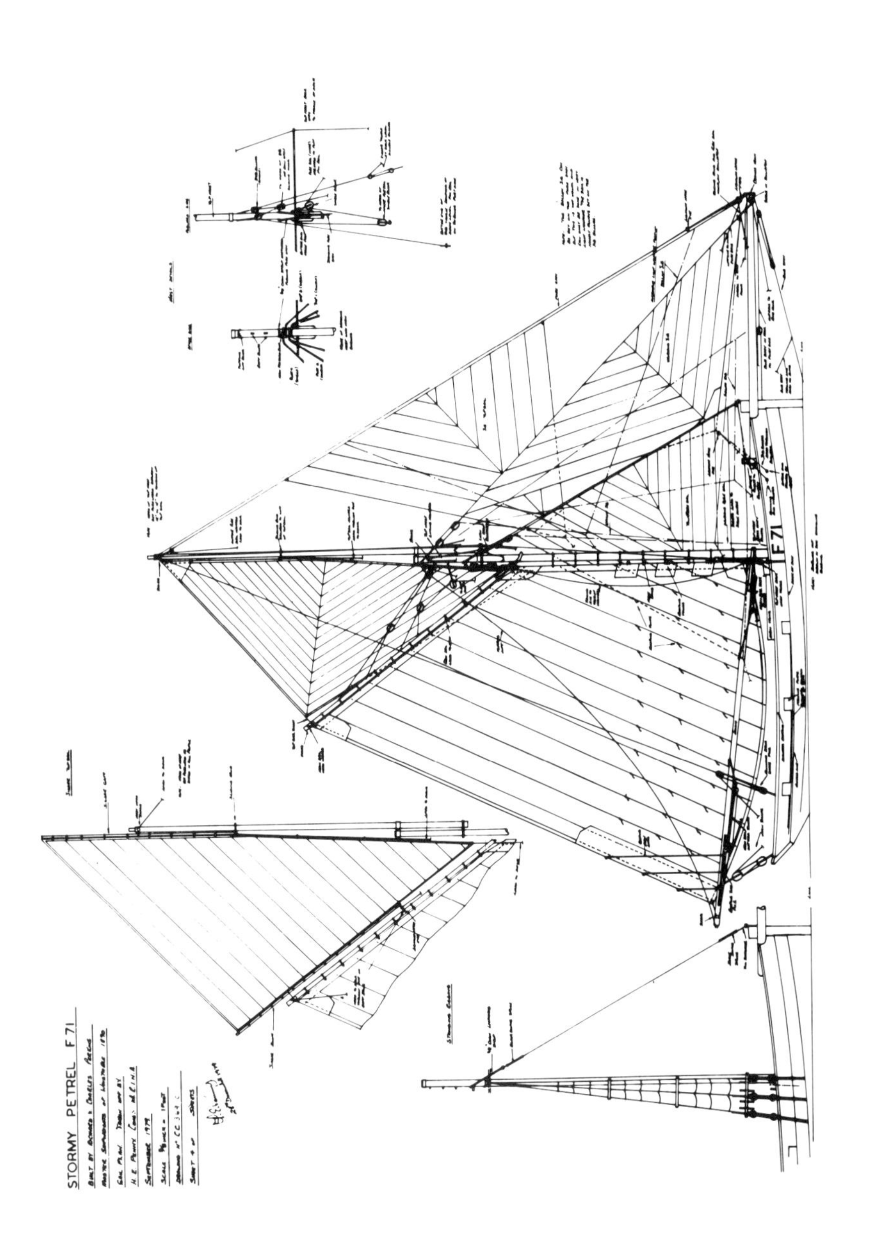


Sail plan of *Stormy Petrel*. (Ted Penny)

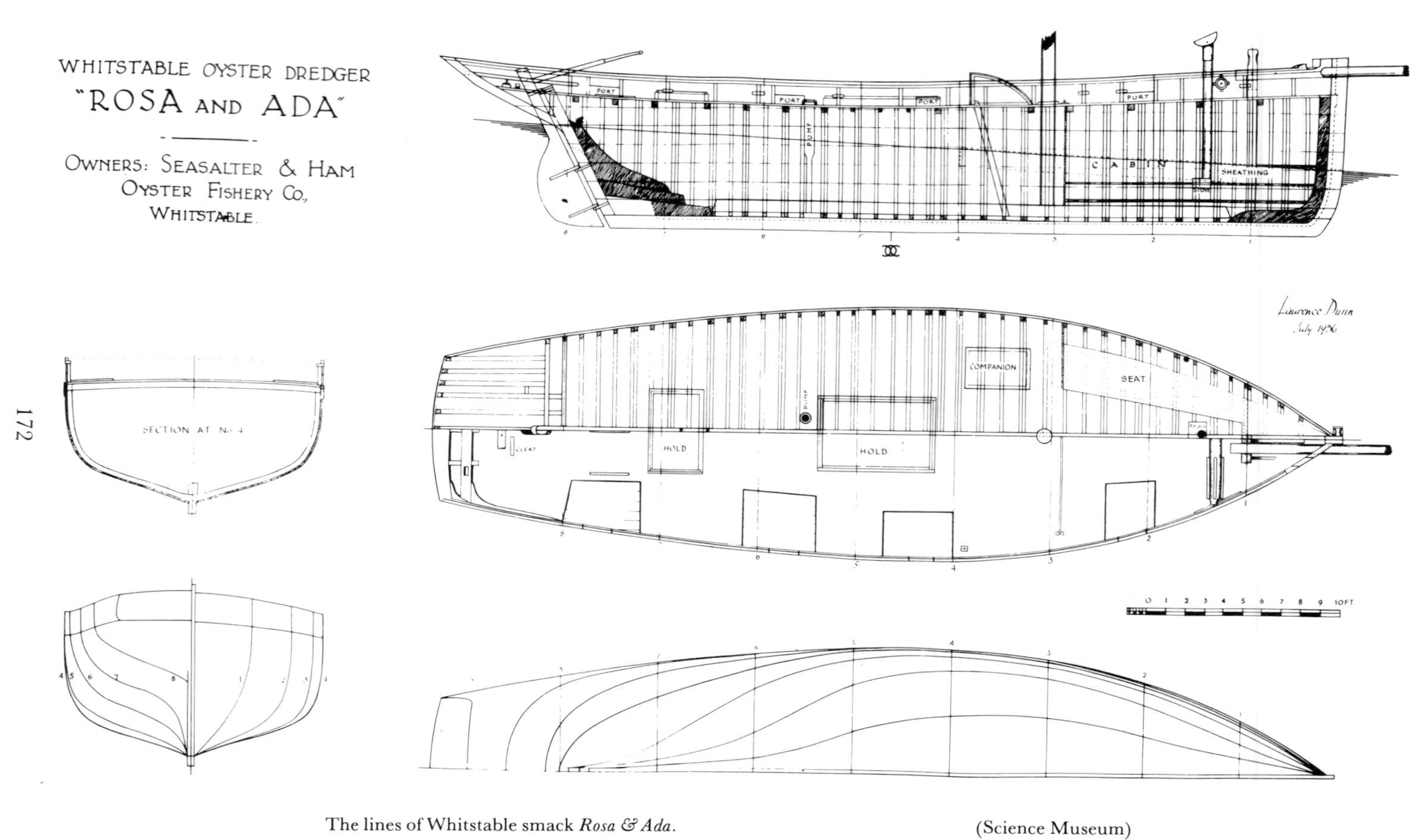


The lines of Whitstable smack *Rosa & Ada*. (Science Museum)

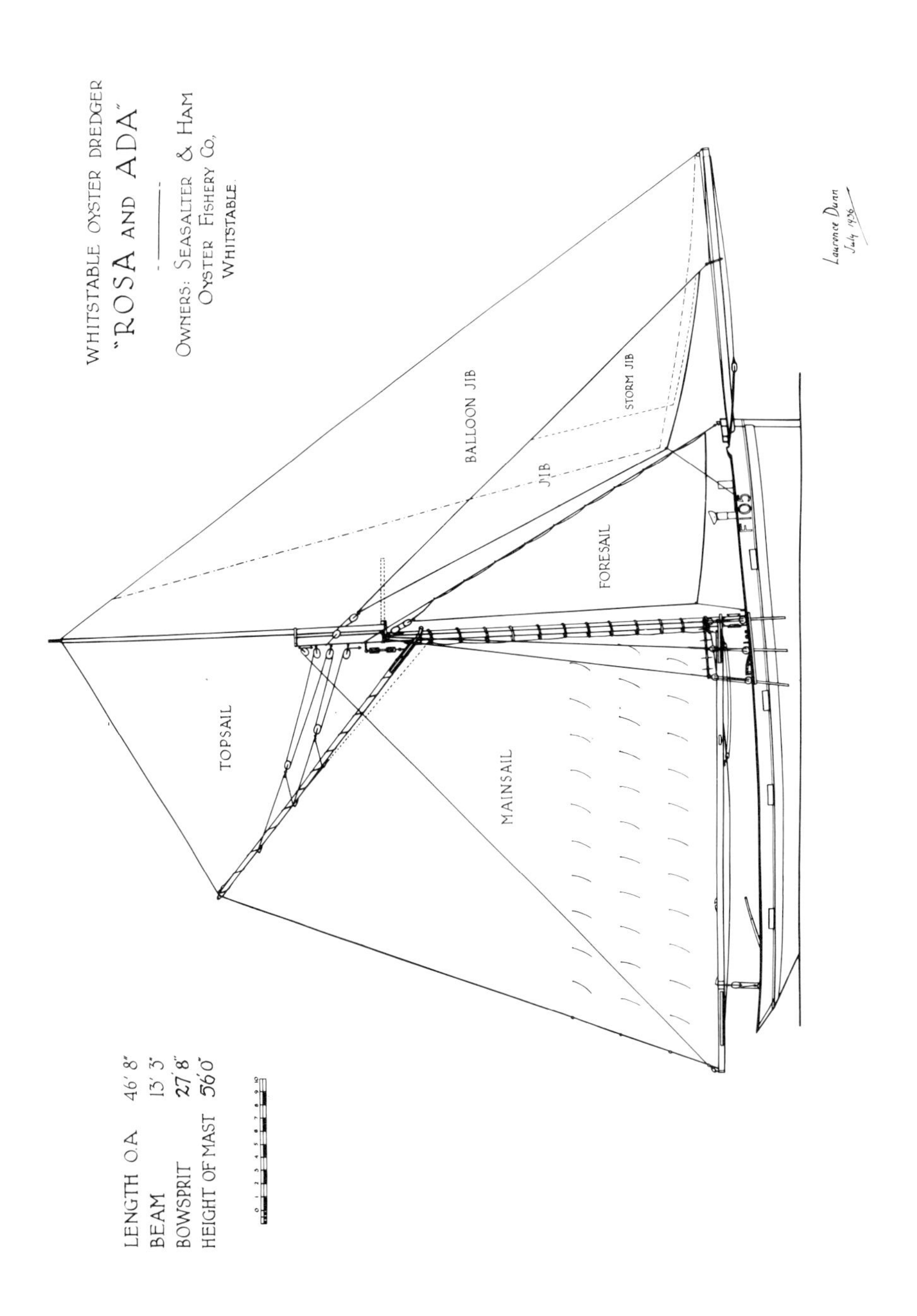


Sail plan of *Rosa & Ada*. (Science Museum)

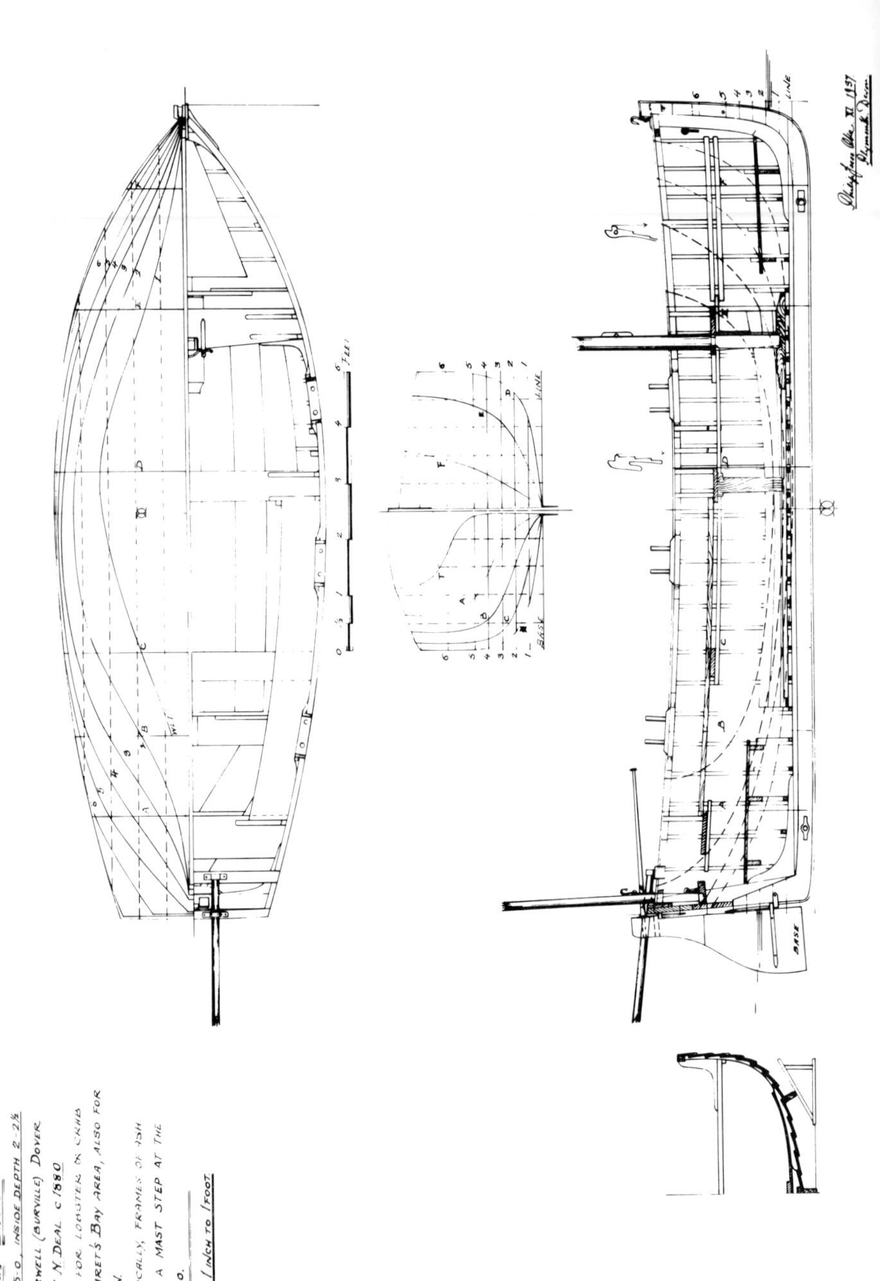


The lines of the Dover beach punt *Argonaut*. (Science Museum)

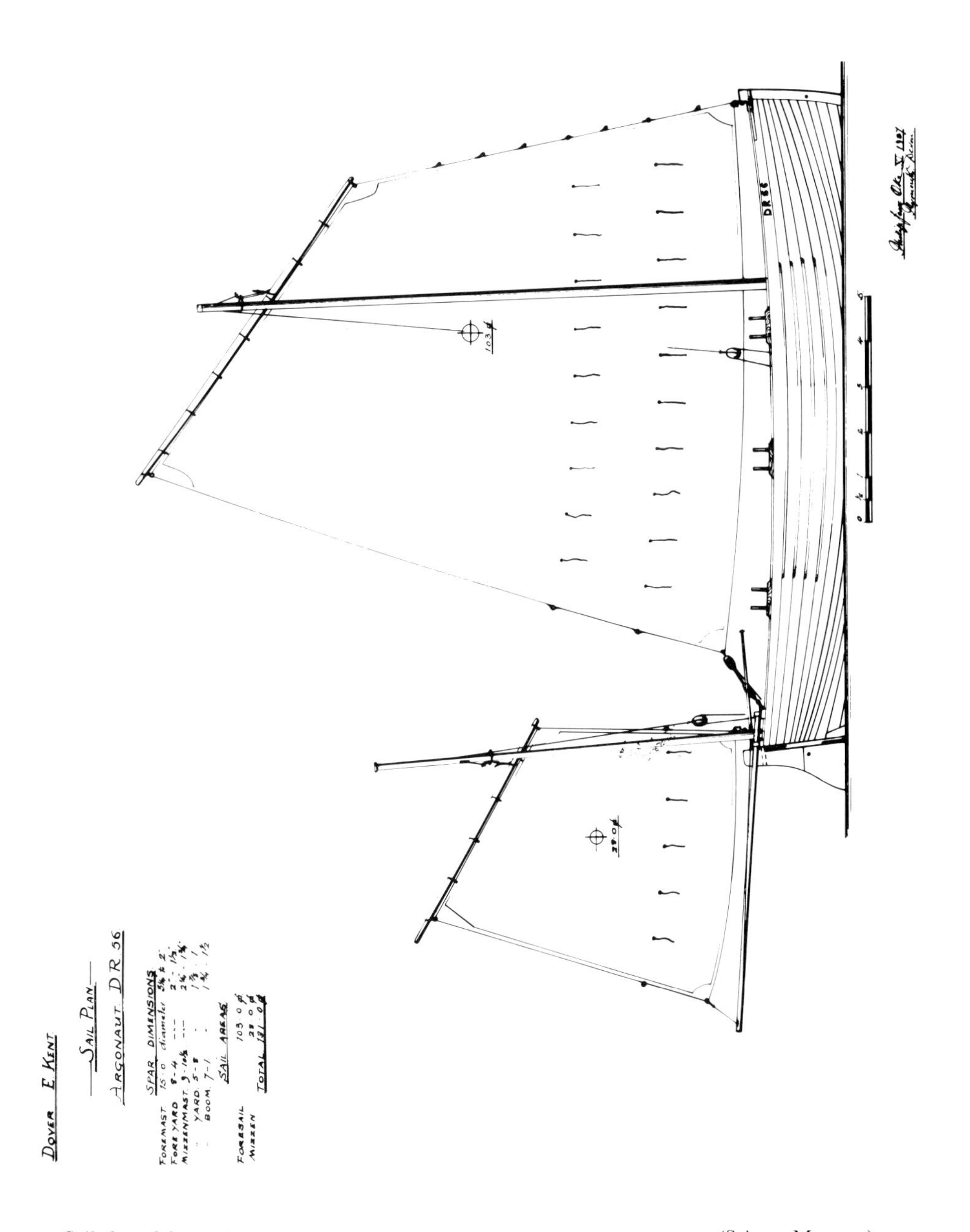


Sail plan of *Argonaut*. (Science Museum)

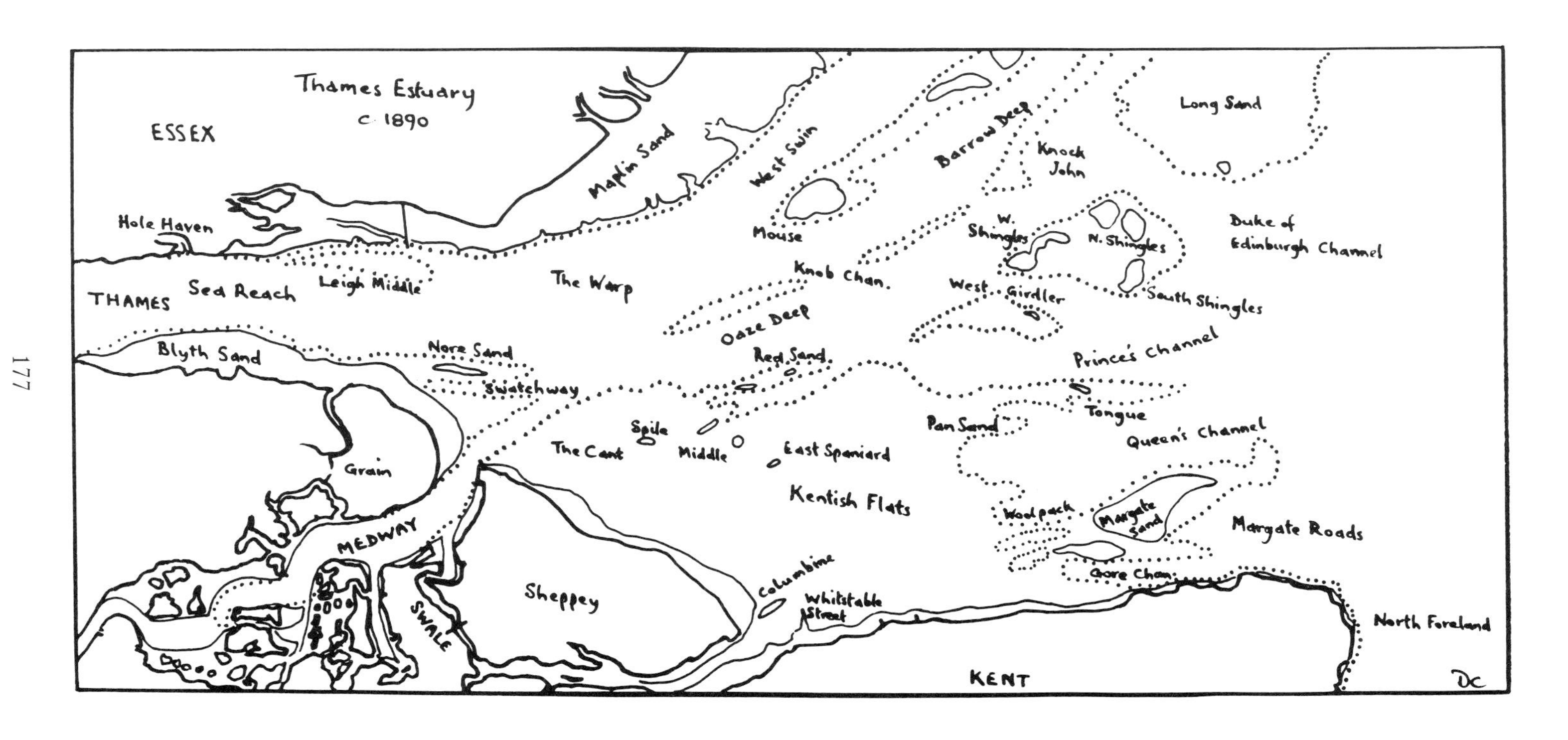

Thames Estuary
c. 1890
ESSEX
Hole Haven
THAMES
Sea Reach
Leigh Middle
Maplin Sand
The Warp
West Swin
Barrow Deep
Knock John
Long Sand
Mouse
W. Shingles
N. Shingles
Duke of Edinburgh Channel
Knob Chan.
West Girdler
South Shingles
Blyth Sand
Nore Sand
Swatchway
Oaze Deep
Red Sand
Prince's Channel
Tongue
Pan Sand
Queen's Channel
Spile
The Cant
Middle
East Spaniard
Grain
Kentish Flats
Woolpack
Margate Sand
Margate Roads
MEDWAY
Gore Chan.
Sheppey
Columbine
Whitstable Street
SWALE
North Foreland
KENT

# INDEX

## LARGE FORMAT PICTORIAL PAPERBACKS

**ARE YOU BEING SERVED, MADAM? by Molly Proctor.** ISBN 3174. £3.50.
**AVIATION IN KENT by Robin J. Brooks.** ISBN 681. £2.95.
**BEFORE AND AFTER THE HURRICANE IN AND AROUND CANTERBURY by Paul Crampton.** ISBN 3387. £3.50.
**THE CANTERBURY BLITZ by Paul Crampton.** ISBN 3441. £9.95.
**EAST KENT FROM THE AIR by John Guy.** ISBN 3158. £3.50.
**EAST SUSSEX RAILWAYS IN OLD POSTCARDS by Kevin Robertson.** ISBN 3220. £3.50.
**GEORGE BARGEBRICK Esq. by Richard-Hugh Perks.** ISBN 479. £4.50.
**GOUDHURST: A Pictorial History by John T. Wilson, M.A.** ISBN 3026. £2.95.
**HEADCORN: A Pictorial History by the Headcorn Local History Society.** ISBN 3271. £3.50.
**KENT TOWN CRAFTS by Richard Filmer.** ISBN 584. £2.95.
**THE LIFE AND ART OF ONE MAN by Dudley Pout.** ISBN 525. £2.95.
**MORE PICTURES OF RAINHAM by Barbara Mackay Miller.** ISBN 3298. £3.50.
**THE MOTOR BUS SERVICES OF KENT AND EAST SUSSEX — A brief history by Eric Baldock.** ISBN 959. £4.95.
**OLD BROADSTAIRS by Michael David Mirams.** ISBN 3115. £3.50.
**OLD CHATHAM: A THIRD PICTURE BOOK by Philip MacDougall.** ISBN 3190. £3.50.
**OLD FAVERSHAM by Arthur Percival.** ISBN 3425. £3.50.
**OLD GILLINGHAM by Philip MacDougall.** ISBN 3328. £3.50.
**OLD MAIDSTONE'S PUBLIC HOUSES by Irene Hales.** ISBN 533. £2.95.
**OLD MAIDSTONE Vol.2 by Irene Hales.** ISBN 38X. £2.50.
**OLD MAIDSTONE Vol.3 by Irene Hales.** ISBN 3336. £3.50.
**OLD MARGATE by Michael David Mirams.** ISBN 851. £3.50.
**OLD PUBS OF TUNBRIDGE WELLS & DISTRICT by Keith Hetherington and Alun Griffiths.** ISBN 300X. £3.50.
**OLD SANDWICH by Julian Arnold and Andrew Aubertin.** ISBN 673. £2.95.
**OLD TONBRIDGE by Don Skinner.** ISBN 398. £2.50.
**PEMBURY IN THE PAST by Mary Standen.** ISBN 916. £2.95.
**A PICTORIAL STUDY OF ALKHAM PARISH by Susan Lees and Roy Humphreys.** ISBN 3034. £2.95.
**A PICTORIAL STUDY OF HAWKINGE PARISH by Roy Humphreys.** ISBN 328X. £3.50.
**A PICTUREBOOK OF OLD RAINHAM by Barbara Mackay Miller.** ISBN 606. £3.50.
**REMINISCENCES OF OLD CRANBROOK by Joe Woodwock.** ISBN 331X. £3.50.
**ROCHESTER FROM OLD PHOTOGRAPHS** — see under hardbacks.
**THOMAS SIDNEY COOPER OF CANTERBURY by Brian Stewart.** ISBN 762. £2.95.
**WEST KENT FROM THE AIR by John Guy.** ISBN 3166. £3.50.

## STANDARD SIZE PAPERBACKS

**BIRDS OF KENT: A Review of their Status and Distribution by the Kent Ornithological Society.** ISBN 800. £6.95.

**BIRDWATCHING IN KENT by Don Taylor.** ISBN 932. £4.50.

**THE CHATHAM DOCKYARD STORY by Philip MacDougall.** ISBN 3301. £6.95.

**CHIDDINGSTONE — AN HISTORICAL EXPLORATION by Jill Newton.** ISBN 940. £1.95.

**A CHRONOLOGY OF ROCHESTER by Brenda Purle.** ISBN 851. £1.50.

**COBHAM.** Published for Cobham Parish Council. ISBN 3123. £1.00.

**CRIME AND CRIMINALS IN VICTORIAN KENT by Adrian Gray.** ISBN 967. £3.95.

**CURIOUS KENT by John Vigar.** ISBN 878. £1.95.

**CYCLE TOURS OF KENT by John Guy.** No. 1: Medway, Gravesend, Sittingbourne and Sheppey. ISBN 517. £1.50.

**DOVER REMEMBERED by Jessie Elizabeth Vine.** ISBN 819. £3.95.

**EXPLORING KENT CHURCHES by John E. Vigar.** ISBN 3018. £3.95.

**EXPLORING SUSSEX CHURCHES by John E. Vigar.** ISBN 3093. £3.95.

**FLIGHT IN KENT.** ISBN 3085. £1.95.

**FROM MOTHS TO MERLINS: The History of West Malling Airfield by Robin J. Brooks.** ISBN 3239. £4.95.

**THE GHOSTS OF KENT by Peter Underwood.** ISBN 86X. £3.95.

**A HISTORY OF CHATHAM GRAMMAR SCHOOL FOR GIRLS, 1907-1982 by Audrey Perkyns.** ISBN 576. £1.95.

**KENT AIRFIELDS IN THE BATTLE OF BRITAIN by the Kent Aviation Historical Research Society.** ISBN 3247. £4.95.

**KENT COUNTRY CHURCHES by James Antony Syms.** ISBN 3131. £4.50.

**KENT COUNTRY CHURCHES CONTINUED by James Antony Syms.** ISBN 314X. £5.95.

**KENT COUNTRY CHURCHES CONCLUDED by James Antony Syms.** ISBN 345X. £5.95.

**KENT INNS AND SIGNS by Michael David Mirams.** ISBN 3182. £3.95.

**LET'S EXPLORE THE RIVER DARENT by Frederick Wood.** ISBN 770. £1.95.

**LULLINGSTONE PARK: THE EVOLUTION OF A MEDIAEVAL DEER PARK by Susan Pittman.** ISBN 703. £3.95.

**PENINSULA ROUND (The Hoo Peninsula) by Des Worsdale.** ISBN 568. £1.50.

**REAL ALE PUBS IN KENT by CAMRA in Kent.** ISBN 3263. Was £1.95. Now 95p.

**SAINT ANDREW'S CHURCH, DEAL by Gregory Holyoake.** ISBN 835. 95p.

**SHORNE: The History of a Kentish Village by A.F. Allen.** ISBN 3204. £4.95.

**SIR GARRARD TYRWHITT-DRAKE AND THE COBTREE ESTATE, MAIDSTONE by Elizabeth Melling B.A.** ISBN 3344. £1.50.

**SITTINGBOURNE & KEMSLEY LIGHT RAILWAY STOCKBOOK AND GUIDE.** ISBN 843. 95p.

**STEAM IN MY FAMILY by John Newton.** ISBN 3417. £4.95.

**STOUR VALLEY WALKS from Canterbury to Sandwich by Christopher Donaldson.** ISBN 991. £1.95.

**TALES OF VICTORIAN HEADCORN** — see under hardbacks.

**WADHURST: Town of the High Weald by Alan Savidge and Oliver Mason.** ISBN 3352. £5.95.

**WHERE NO FLOWERS GROW by George Glazebrook.** ISBN 3379. £2.50.

**THE WORKHOUSE AND THE WEALD by Dorothy Hatcher.** ISBN 3360. £4.95.